XI

A STUDY IN POWER

KERRY BROWN

ICON

Published in the UK in 2022 by Icon Books Ltd
Omnibus Business Centre, 39–41 North Road, London N7 9DP
email: info@iconbooks.com • www.iconbooks.com

Sold in the UK, Europe and Asia
by Faber & Faber Ltd, Bloomsbury House, 74–77 Great Russell Street,
London WC1B 3DA or their agents

Distributed in the UK, Europe and Asia
by Grantham Book Services, Trent Road, Grantham NG31 7XQ

Distributed in the USA
by Publishers Group West, 1700 Fourth Street, Berkeley, CA 94710

Distributed in Canada
by Publishers Group Canada, 76 Stafford Street, Unit 300,
Toronto, Ontario M6J 2S1

Distributed in Australia and New Zealand
by Allen & Unwin Pty Ltd, PO Box 8500, 83 Alexander Street,
Crows Nest, NSW 2065

Distributed in South Africa
by Jonathan Ball, Office B4, The District, 41 Sir Lowry Road,
Woodstock 7925

Distributed in India by Penguin Books India,
7th Floor, Infinity Tower – C, DLF Cyber City, Gurgaon 122002, Haryana

ISBN: 978-178578-808-6

Typeset in Haarlemmer by Marie Doherty

Printed and bound in Great Britain
by Clays Ltd, Elcograf S.p.A.

To Andrew Beale, my first teacher of Chinese,
who lives with the consequences every day.

Contents

Preface

Imagine that you stop someone on the street in Europe or the US and ask them to name the most powerful person in the world. They might say the US president, or the founders of Facebook or Amazon. The more eclectic might suggest the Pope, or the owner of a news empire, like Rupert Murdoch.

In recent years, more and more people might say the current leader of China, Xi Jinping. As recognition of this, in 2017, the *Economist* placed Xi directly next to the then American President Donald Trump, arguing that the former had become more powerful than the latter. Despite this, few feel they really know what sort of a person and politician Xi is, nor that they understand much about the country he leads.

People believe Xi is powerful for three main reasons. The first, and most obvious, is that the economic and military capability of the People's Republic has come from the margins in the 1980s to being at the global forefront by the late 2010s. Barring disaster, some time before 2030, Xi's country is expected to overtake the US and become the world's largest economy. Proof of how much this rattled the world's uncontested superpower at the time was that, after years of dismissing China's hopes of ever getting to such a position, Trump became fixated on this new great competitor. This was certainly not a comfortable place for China to occupy – but in many ways being viewed so closely and jealously by Washington was the highest form of flattery for Beijing. The fact that the world's most powerful nation felt threatened by China showed that the nation mattered. Xi's country was no longer in the margins.

The second reason is that Xi himself seems to exemplify power. It exudes from him almost like a physical force. Since his rise to the head of the Communist Party in 2012, a body that enjoys a monopoly of organised political control in the country, he has cleared away all possible internal competition. Evidence of his desire for control is everywhere, and sometimes shocking in its detail. With the use of new technology and new messaging, and with China on the cusp of being the greatest global nation, Xi symbolises this ambition in the flesh. He speaks and acts like a leader with endless confidence. Even if this is an act, it is an effective one.

But the third reason is about the context of that power. Questioned, tested and often even humiliated in their own political environments, leaders of democracies in the West might look at Xi's position and, perhaps, feel the slightest tinge of envy. With control of the party he leads, Xi has levers over the media, the military, business and practically every other part of society that other leaders could only dream of. He leads the country as a skilled conductor leads an orchestra, where the obedient players are all on message and there is no sign of dissent.

This capacity, however, was not built overnight. Xi is powerful, but much of that power is contextual. A huge amount of it derives not from him but from the political party he leads. He has also had the luck to inherit leadership of the Communist Party and the country at a time when a number of different developments have come together. Now, after decades of sacrifice and effort, is the time of feasting. Technology, the economy and the confused situation of the outside world have created a vast historic opportunity in China's favour. The Communist Party was brought to power by Mao in 1949 and, after some disastrous adventures along the way, made stronger and sustainable by Deng Xiaoping, Jiang Zemin and Hu Jintao. All of these leaders have contributed significantly to the position that Xi is now in, and to his good fortune. Xi's power did not come from nowhere.

What has perhaps most unsettled Western commentators is not so much China's prominence but the way it has developed more quickly than anyone ever expected. The country has always been acknowledged by the rest of the world as being important. But half a century ago, in the 1970s, Maoist

China was introspective, diplomatically isolated, economically undeveloped, largely rural and regarded as a place that would always struggle just to survive. Today, China looks like another country. The strongest link between these periods is the party, the entity that now has 95 million members led by Xi. It alone provides the common point between these very different eras. To work out how these two Chinas are part of the same story, showing the same ambition, one has to start with the role of the party, and understand Xi's role within it. Xi Jinping and the Communist Party need to be seen as inseparable entities, Using unique Chinese sources, some of which have never been properly analysed in the English language before, this book attempts to do that. It also shows how extraordinary the party has been as a vehicle for Chinese modernisation and nationalism, and how formidable Xi has proved as the director of these forces.

Make no bones about it, because of the dramatic new situation China is in, Xi is possibly the one leader out of the current global heads of state that will have the greatest impact on the present and the future of the world and its development. The mere fact that he is in charge of a fifth of humanity is enough to justify this claim. But it is also merited by the fact that his country now stands on the cusp of finally achieving modernity on Chinese terms. This is a wholly new story, never seen in our times.

While Xi is the symbol of these forces of national rejuvenation and ambition, we should not get carried away and start to regard him as their creator. Chinese people desire better quality of life regardless of what their current political leaders say. Part of Xi's effectiveness has been in crafting messages and policies domestically that speak to the growing middle class and their hopes and ambitions in ways that keep them onside. Failure to see this factor clearly has been one of the key reasons why many outside China have dismissed him merely as a dictator and autocrat. He is a far more complex leader than that, even if elements of his leadership style do fall under those descriptions. The paradox of Xi Jinping is that in many ways he as an individual person does not count – rather it is the body he represents, the Communist Party of China, with its history, its sense of mission, its complete control over all organised political life in China and its view of humanity, time and social life that is important. As the leader of this body, Xi matters. Conveying his achievements and politics in ways that properly acknowledge this balance between the individual and the group they lead, and therefore have power through, is crucial.

Whatever one thinks of Xi and the system he operates in – something this book will try to explain – one thing is irrefutable. The decisions he is making and the direction his country goes in will have a massive impact on the global economy, on climate change, security and human development. Everyone who cares about these things, wherever they happen to be, needs to know about Xi and have an interest in who he is, what he is doing and why. To understand our world today, it is vital to know about the leader of the world's most influential economy, one that is deeply integrated into global supply chains that reach into our homes, one that will have a decisive impact on whether humanity is able to conquer climate change and clean up its environment and one whose leadership is shaping the most fundamental geopolitical balancing between East and West seen in modern times. For those who are interested in the affairs of the modern world, understanding Xi is crucial.

CHAPTER ONE

Xi Jinping:
The Enigma of Chinese Power

Two decades ago, I was a British diplomat serving in Beijing. During an earlier stay, I had become aware of the leadership compound that lay beside the vast Forbidden City in the heart of the capital but had never managed to set foot in the place. However, during the visit of a senior British politician around the turn of the millennium, I was invited to accompany them to this hallowed place. The experience was disorientating. Driving through the chaotic and crushing traffic in the city centre, our embassy car swept into a side gate. It was as though we had disappeared into another world. Peace reigned. Beyond the security guards at the entrance, there was no one in sight. Classical buildings stood by tranquil lakes. The grass looked as though it had been cut by scissors. Everything was still, calm – the opposite of the metropolis, one of the largest and most congested in the world, we had left outside. The place exuded an intangible sense of power.

In modern China, power is largely seen as something real, which certain people possess and others don't, but which has an air of mystery about it. One of the numerous 'givens' for Western journalists covering Chinese elite politics over the past few decades is that those at the top of the ruling Communist Party of China have an abundance of it. There are not many of these people. The assumption is that they are laden with vast surfeits of this thing called 'power'; they can run riot with it, annexing everything around them at their individual will. But is this really the case? Does 'power' have such a common currency and such consistent characteristics? Two of the finest historians of the modern country's events, Fred Teiwes and Warren Sun, went to great lengths in their meticulous account of the final years of Mao's rule to say that, while everyone can agree that he did have massive authority, 'things were more complicated'.[1]

One source of confusion about structures of power in China is the idea that leaders today are little different from the emperors who led the country during its long imperial history until 1912. Like them, Mao, Deng and Xi are similar to modern gods, ruling with absolute authority over their subjects, enjoying an almost semi-divine status. It is questionable whether Chinese emperors did in fact have such powers.

The vast majority of their subjects probably spent their lives completely oblivious as to who was reigning over them. But the China that Xi Jinping lives in and rules today is not the same as the Chinas that existed before. Ironically, for all the claims about the great antiquity of Chinese history, the People's Republic of China is not yet a hundred years old. It is a young state. Places such as the United Kingdom, France and even the United States and Australia can make claims to some sort of cohesive national narrative going back at least 150 years, and in some cases much further. Their governance structures and administrations are often much better established than those of the People's Republic in Beijing, which only took form in 1949. While the concept of 'China' is, on the surface, a very ancient one – and there certainly is overlap between the geographical reach of predecessor states and the current one (particularly the expansionist Qing era, 1644–1912) – one could claim that much of the country we see today has been created since the Second World War, and in many cases even more recently. Power is moulded both by what it is directed at and what it is intended to have influence over. Like water, it changes its shape depending on what it strikes against. Xi Jinping's powers are therefore different to those of China's leaders prior to 1949 because the place he exerts power over did not exist then.

Even after 1949, each core leader has had bespoke styles and kinds of power, as much because of the changing economic and political situation of their country, as anything to do with them personally. Mao Zedong, who ruled from 1949–76, was the great founder, a figure of God-like proportions. His successor, Deng Xiaoping, who was leader from 1978–89, was more prosaic and strategic – history will probably judge him as being much more effective than Mao in creating sustainable outcomes. After Deng's era came Jiang Zemin, who ruled as party head from 1989 to 2002. He presented a more extrovert, oft-mocked leadership style, despite the fact that with his slippery, often buffoonish character he stabilised the country after the 1989 Tiananmen Square uprising and recommitted to play a role in the global economy through finally joining the World Trade Organization in 2001. Hu Jintao, the faceless, egoless successor to Jiang, mastered the art of making China a vast factory for economic growth, quadrupling the size of its GDP over the decade he was in office from 2002 to 2012, an unrivalled achievement in modern history. After all of these leaders came Xi. He has been talked of, by no less a figure than President Obama, as the leader who has most quickly and effectively consolidated his position since the time of Mao. What links these different figures is that they worked within the Communist tradition of governance. Maybe Xi is the most powerful of them all. But this is because China has greater significance as a country now than it did in the past. It is not because Xi has some kind of magic quality. The reasons for his power are very prosaic – China has more money, more technology, more military equipment than ever before, and this is in comparison to a West that is weakening. There is nothing mysterious in any of this.

Xi and his colleagues certainly see themselves as occupying a phase in a continuous project that started in 1949, one where their actions are only possible because of the achievements of their predecessors. Xi himself has made it clear that the idea of repudiating Mao will not happen, at least under his watch. For Xi, without the Chairman, there would be no China as it exists today, in pole position to achieve its dreams of modernity and to overtake the US to become the world's largest economy within the next decade. If Xi is the most powerful leader of the country since Mao, this is because of the systems and structures, and achievements, that arose from the hard work of his predecessors. He himself doesn't deny this. He will see the country achieve things that Mao dreamt of but could never realise – his country having a navy with more vessels than the US, one that is able to speak back as an equal to American presidents, one that has eradicated absolute poverty. This sense of belonging to a great tradition of Communist Party leadership since 1949 in China, therefore, is crucial in understanding Xi as a political figure.

Xi's power also exists to serve a purpose. This is not about his own individual aims. It is about the great objective of the

Communist Party to build a strong, rich country. This transcends specific leaders, and particular eras. The Communist Party is an atheist organisation. But that doesn't mean it has no faith. Belief in the almost semi-mystical entity of 'China' with its spiritual import, its cultural richness and human vastness is the great overarching creed that has prevailed since 1949, and it has roots that extend far further back than this. Making this China powerful, strong and central in world affairs once more, as it had been in the distant past, is the key mission. Xi is a servant of that greater mission, almost in the same way the Pope leads the Catholic Church in its mission to deliver humanity to the Kingdom of Heaven. The main difference is that for Xi's faith, that kingdom will be found on this earth. Of all the sources of Xi's power, this one is the most potent.

The nature of the leadership he practises needs to be interpreted as serving these larger, longer-term aims related to faith in the great nation. If we want to describe Xi as an autocrat, it is because he is serving autocratic aims. There must be total fidelity to the great cause of making China great again. This is a jealous objective, and one that does not permit any vagueness nor any lack of commitment. Xi's leadership style can be seen as almost designed to recognise this. The autocratic cause creates the leadership style, not the other way around. This is a crucial issue, if one truly wants to understand what is happening in China today.

On more mundane levels, Xi's powers also need to be seen as circumscribed and limited. The Communist Party of China does not merely have a strong guiding, nationalist faith, but also a strong identity and ethos. Most of this was created long before Xi even became a member in 1974. To succeed in it at any level means adhering to this pre-determined set of rules and customs. You become as the party wants you, rather than you making the party become like you. As scholar Zheng Yongnian pointed out, contemporary China does indeed have an emperor – but it is in the form of the organisation of the Communist Party, rather than a human individual.[2]

In terms of the context of Xi's power, and how one can compare him to predecessors like Mao, we have to recognise that the country that he rules over today has radically transformed from the one that existed only four decades ago. Socially, culturally, economically and in its physical appearance, it is almost a different country. Change itself is the great constant of modern China – change in terms of how people live, what work they do and how fast this change has occurred. The sole constant is the fact that the Communist Party has continued to have a monopoly on power. Beyond that, everything else seems to have been remodelled.

Even an outsider like myself can testify to this. In the mid-1990s I lived in a fairly typical provincial city in China for two years. It had no high-rise buildings, was served by often pockmarked roads and its central area was dominated by a charming, chaotic and ramshackle old city where temples nestled beside shops, merchants' houses and tombstone sellers. Returning to this place in the early 2000s after a few years' absence, I was wholly unable to find my way around. Literally nothing remained to orientate me. A vast, shiny new airport had been built, as had a new museum about ten times the size of the old one, with huge halls displaying dinosaurs, furnished with interactive, hi-tech teaching aids. New civic buildings dominated one part of the city. There were skyscrapers everywhere, glittering in the sun. The roads were pristine, with glitzy, expensive imported cars driving along them. Only after much searching could I find at least one of the old temples, turning the corner of a huge new boulevard running south through where the old city once was. There it stood, almost stranded in a sea of change, its doors and courtyard recognisable. I found this strangely moving and reassuring. But after gazing at it for a while, I realised that even this place had experienced an extensive makeover.

This is not a unique incidence. Change has infected every part of China. It means that the kinds of tasks and the sorts of objectives the leadership – by which I mean the institution rather than specific personalities – must fulfil have also changed. And yet, as we will see, a choice has been made by Xi and those around him, deep in the party, to maintain this almost old-fashioned, highly unified leadership model. It is as though the Communist Party were like that former temple I recognised in among the sea of change the day I revisited my old home – a focal point to orientate and reassure people that they have not strayed on to a totally different planet. In a country undergoing this extent of transformation, and with the impact of all its technological advances, the commitment to a single, authoritative centralising figure has remained the default. In Xi's China, the party is not back to the future, but back to the past. In every other aspect of Chinese life, the reverse is true, with things becoming more complex, diverse and renewed by the day. To opt for a leadership like this has a simple logic: in a world where everything else is pervaded by change, transformation and transition, the party and the party alone is the great bastion of stability and permanence. To coin a phrase, in the kingdom of change, the changeless one is King!

How deliberate a construct is the Xi political persona, bearing in mind the context of leadership customs and the party's custodianship of a strong, enduring identity and ethos? Acknowledging this is not to the denigration of Xi's individual political skills; far from it. In February 2018, James Fallows wrote in the *Atlantic* that Xi is an autocrat, not a reformer; but while much of the Western world seems to be consumed by fears that they are seeing the rise of yet another terrifying Asian dictator, there is little recognition that when dealing with a potential opponent, a good place to start is by recognising their strengths.[3] At a dinner in London some years back, an American sitting next to me airily declared that, of course, 'Xi Jinping is evil.' It was hard to work out what they meant by that, beyond seeking an easy way to consign him to a pigeonhole from which he could be easily dismissed. Xi's political convictions might be considered problematic, along with the policies his government has implemented that have affected minorities, such as the population in Xinjiang. These are often profoundly concerning and hard to understand. But merely dismissing Xi Jinping's success as a leader means one is not seeing him clearly enough to fully engage with the challenges he and his country pose. Xi is a problem for the world not because he is some old-style Communist dictator playing by the rule book of Stalin and Mao, but because he is an effective leader of a modernised economy, a modernising military and a powerful, modern state. Dismissing him with a lazy label helps no one.

That he has succeeded in a political system which is deeply disliked by many in the West, means that, in today's world, even a bald statement asserting that Xi is a hugely effective and talented leader is likely to bring massive opprobrium upon the head of whoever makes such an assessment. At a time of deep divisions between left and right in America, hard attitudes and policies towards China are one of the few things that unites both sides. Republican Mario Rubio in the US has called

China a 'genocidal regime',[4] while in the same year, President Joe Biden said that the country is a 'threat to democratic way of life'.[5] In Europe, too, the country has moved from being seen as a partner to a 'systemic rival' – a phrase used by the European Union in 2019.[6] There are even darker and murkier issues of potential xenophobia about Western uneasiness towards such a culturally different power becoming predominant for the first time in modern history. As Covid-19 spread across the world from China in 2020, the lamentable incidences of people of Chinese heritage being abused and attacked in the UK, US and Australia increased rapidly.[7] The combination of these attitudes created an often toxic brew. It also raises uncomfortable questions about how much the response to China's new prominence is about the country itself, and how much is about the already existing fears, prejudices and obsessions of those observing and witnessing this new power.

In this chaotic and confusing situation, we can see evidence of Xi's political skills – things he did well regardless of our views of the system he works in. He managed to emerge from the messy transition period between him and his predecessor Hu Jintao with enough space around him to build what he wanted. Unlike Hu, whose stint in power was reportedly blighted by the persistent interference of the man he had succeeded, Jiang Zemin, Xi seemed to have his hands on all the levers of power from the word go. He was head of the party and the military from November 2012 and became president in March 2013 – things Hu had to wait a year or two for in the succession a decade before. He has had an obedient and capable group of colleagues around him, people such as Li Keqiang and the formidable Wang Qishan, who have offered no distraction from the leadership persona that he wanted to construct. The former had no power base of his own, while the latter was already too old to pose much of a long-term threat. By focussing on anti-corruption and building up rule by law to protect commercial rights while ceding no ground to political opponents, Xi was able to discipline the greatest threat to him – contenders in the party and its high-level leadership who felt they, not Xi, should have the top spot. Most importantly, with concepts like the 'China Dream', an idea issued by the party in 2012 to refer to the vision of the country being powerful and rich in the next decade, and Xi's key foreign policy idea, the Belt and Road Initiative (all of which will be explained in more detail later), he has been able to craft a narrative that grants meaning and purpose to the context of his leadership and explains how it serves in delivering the great overarching political vision described above – the creation of a powerful, great China. The country now has vast wealth and a new capacity, accrued since the time of Deng Xiaopeng in the 1980s. It has the economic capital to be able to take decisive action today. These financial gains were not for their own sake, but for something more. Xi may well be the lucky man who found himself in the right place at the right time, when the country not only has a nationalist vision, but also has the means to make this a reality as never before.

No matter where a politician works, or which environment they are in, making the most of good fortune and opportunities is a key ability. Just like a football player on a pitch who has the chance at a shot at goal, the difference between a good player and a great one is how many of these opportunities are converted to goals. Xi is well known as a keen football fan. Despite the terrible record of the Chinese national football team, at one point in 2011, immediately before coming to power, he spoke of the three Chinese dreams: for the country to compete once again in the World Cup finals (its only other participation took place in 2002), to host the World Cup and to be World Cup winners.[8] He has shown that, like the football stars he so admires, and successful politicians everywhere, he knows how to use that luck. He is a supreme opportunist, a convertor of chances into goals. What differentiates him from other contemporary national leaders is the sheer scale of the opportunity he has been given.

Xi has had his fair share of luck since 2012. There were a few years when it seemed that everything was going his way. The world was distracted by turmoil in the Middle East and Russia's annexation of the Crimea. The US was being consumed by culture wars between left and right, which

13

culminated in the brutal 2016 presidential campaign that pitted Donald Trump against Hillary Clinton. Europe was in a seemingly perpetual crisis as it fought first with the fallout of the 2009 Eurozone crisis and then the rise of populist political parties in countries such as Italy, France and Germany. The terrorist group ISIS was looming as the biggest security threat since 9/11. But in 2015, when the central Chinese government fumbled the response to a collapse in the Shanghai Stock Exchange, impoverishing the all-important middle class who were the main holders of accounts in the country, it seemed that Xi's luck was starting to run out. The 2017 election of Donald Trump to the White House and the start of his administration's sustained pushback on China resulted in a trade war and the imposition of tariffs; and then the catastrophic Covid-19 pandemic in early 2020 proved Xi's greatest test yet. As the pandemic took hold, the first signs did not augur well. Xi effectively disappeared in late January 2020. As journalist Jamil Anderlini put it in the *Financial Times*, the pandemic was China's Chernobyl, the mismanagement of which in the mid-1980s by the government of the Soviet Union presaged the country's demise. In February 2020, the *Wall Street Journal* published an article declaring that China was 'the sick person of Asia' because of the woes facing it.*

---

* The Chinese government responded by expelling the newspaper's journalists from the country.

And then the pandemic spread throughout the rest of the world. It was no longer a rerun of the SARS (severe acute respiratory syndrome) outbreak of almost two decades earlier that had been restricted to Asia. By April, countries in Europe, America, Australia and elsewhere were starting to become overwhelmed by infections. Around the same time that China, after strict lockdowns and social controls, managed to get on top of the spread of the infection, other nations began to buckle under the strain. Impositions of orders to restrict the free movement of people and shut down society meant that much of the world started to look just as China had. The one difference was that other nations, with their delayed lockdowns, hesitancy to enforce the use of face masks and fierce internal arguments between vaxxers and anti-vaxxers, appeared to be far more incompetent. As transmission rates soared, and deaths tragically rose, China itself became more like an oasis of calm. Residents in the city of Wuhan, where the crisis had started, may initially have been furious at their own leaders. But this frustration was soon replaced by bewildered gratitude, as they saw a US president downplay the disease and then promptly contract it, before trying to prove he was healthy by emerging from hospital while still infectious, to parade up and down in a car to small crowds. The chaos didn't end there. The British prime minister who had told the public the disease was nothing to worry about, and shaken hands with

Covid-19 patients in a hospital, was himself hospitalised by the disease. Compared to this, Chinese leaders seemed the acme of prudence and competence.

Covid-19 is certainly not the sort of opportunity Xi's government may have wanted to prove their administrative prowess. The impact of the pandemic has created a far sharper, more divided world, and one where there are greater levels of antagonism towards the country from other states. But it showed that Xi could deal with a huge emergency arguably more effectively than many of his fellow national leaders, and that he knew how to turn this to domestic political use. This is not to dignify the claims that the whole episode was deliberately concocted by the Chinese government, which belong to the outer reaches of fantasy. After all, if the pandemic had got out of hand in China, as so nearly happened in January 2020, it would have had a devastating effect on Xi and his colleagues.[9] But it proved that Xi could turn a negative event into a positive one, creating political opportunities. By February 2022, according to data collated by Johns Hopkins University in the US, China had had 120,000 infections and 4,800 deaths from the virus since it appeared two years before.[10] (These figures have been disputed by some as dramatically underreported – but were they even several multiples higher they would still fall far short of US or European levels, particularly taking China's size into account.) Although it has a quarter of China's population, by the same date, the US had 74 million infections, and 884,000 deaths.[11] Brutal it might be, but when accused of having disdain for human life, Xi's government could say it had done more to preserve the wellbeing of its citizens during the pandemic than the world's greatest democracy.

How exactly the outside world frames Xi and understands the context of his power matters. As the pandemic spread, I was struck by how long-established narratives about China were brought to the fore, and how increasingly unfit for purpose they were when faced with the complexities of contemporary geopolitics. It was as though we were trying to use the language of Newtonian physics to describe quantum mechanics. A glance across the various portrayals of Xi in much Western (by which I mean North America, Europe and other aligned multi-party democratic systems) media and commentary shows that, since the Covid-19 crisis started, he has received oblique praise, with the BBC in May 2021 calling him a 'consummate political chess player who has cultivated an enigmatic strongman image'.[12] Xi is imputed with super-human powers. His is the hidden hand that creeps into governments, gets close to political leaders and buys up the allegiance of powers across Africa, Latin America and the rest of the world.[13] His Belt and Road Initiative is a master plan for domination and control. He is 'buying' universities as august and long established as that of Cambridge.[14] His is the genius behind companies like telecoms equipment and technology manufacturer Huawei, whose public insistence that they are independent of his government carries no weight among the main experts on the invisible world of cyber espionage, who produce weekly accounts of the terrifyingly effective tricks and deeds that China is undertaking.[15] This is a highly flattering level of influence to grant one man. If even a fraction of this corpus of material were true, it would show that Xi has been by far the most effective of the modern non-Western leaders in rattling the West's self-confidence. If this were a psychological war (and perhaps in some ways it is) then China currently seems to have the advantage.

It is interesting that, while there is a corresponding fear of foreign interference and agitation within China, Xi's domestic language acknowledges that the far greater threat is not from the other nations but from within. The party he belongs to is the target of his most severe dissatisfaction and ire and has been accused of being the greatest source of potential failure if it does not get tougher on itself. In this respect, he is similar to Mao. Even before coming to central power, during his years as party leader in the province of Zhejiang, he was palpably angry at the party's ability to undermine itself through its lack of focus on the larger political vision. At a time when most officials were swimming in narcissism and focussed on material self-enrichment, feathering their own and their wider network's nests, this was not a popular message. But as of 2022, it has proved to be a politically rewarding one. Xi seems to have worked out that the most powerful thing in modern China is to believe in anything at all, at a time when most people merely believe in money.

Whatever 'power' might be, on one thing we can all agree: for Xi it is clearly vital. Where does he believe that his power is derived from? The huge security services under his command? The military that is growing bigger each year? The vast economy his country has built? We can, at best, speculate. But while it is likely he regards these as important instruments for power, they are merely a means to an end. By studying his actions we can learn where he expends most of his energy, time being his most precious asset. Beyond the great effort spent in disciplining and berating the party he leads, what Xi spends most of the rest of his time doing is in telling stories. It is evident that he believes it is by these means that he can reach the real place where he must have influence and authority – the minds and emotion of the people he leads. The Maoist phrase that power grows from the barrel of a gun has become a cliché in modern China. It is also imprecise. Power is not about the gun, but what is in the mind of the person holding that gun. Xi seeks to enact and relate narratives that give Chinese citizens meaningful ways in which the Communist Party relates to their daily lives today. Many of his stories are about the national mission to make the country great again and restore this ancient civilisation to its central role in the world, in ways that transcend politics and which each individual can take part in. This reduces the vast distance between the party's elite and the people on the street. By talking this way, Xi is not the Communist Party leader, but something more akin to a trusty big brother, a father figure or the *Xi Dada** that became popular on Chinese social media around 2014, before the censors grew nervous about its levity and banned it.

When told in China, that story of the country's rise to great power has impact and significance. Outside the country, though, things grow trickier. Here the audience is not Chinese people with their shared symbols, language and habits. The context of the lives of non-Chinese are very different. For this external world, in the era of China's modern rise since the death of Mao in 1976, there have been two broad stories about this complex, ever-evolving country. One version sees the place as some vast ersatz capitalist project, aping Western money-making processes and discourse. If one adopts this storyline, China could be seen as either a potential object of huge material enrichment for companies or, more negatively, as an economic competitor and threat. The alternative story positions China as a hell of human rights abuses and misery,

* Uncle Xi

where the desperate citizens silenced by oppressive state censorship are sending out cries for liberation and help to the outside world. In fact, these two plotlines are not new. From the start of European engagement with Ming-era China, five centuries ago, Jesuits and other Catholic missionaries regarded the country as a vast pool of potential converts to Christianity, and saw themselves as liberating the people from their unenlightened and Godless blindness.* In the late 16th century, the Italian Jesuit Matteo Ricci was the most celebrated of these, a man who lived in China so long that he adopted Chinese dress and mannerisms, and wrote his works in the local language. This sat alongside the mercantile approach, which viewed the place as a source of trade opportunities, and potential wealth creation for outside governments and companies, such as the infamous British East India Company. The latter came to the fore after the First Opium War of 1839–42 when the reigning Qing dynasty was forced to open up to outside trade, at the hands of forces including the British military. These broad narratives of commercial opportunity and the possibility of ideological conversion versus human rights hell have continued like two well-worn train tracks to the present day. And they are, as is obvious even on this bald retelling, in increasingly overt

---

* Many of these missionaries came to have a deep knowledge and complex appreciation of the culture they had been sent to transform.

conflict; if one believes a place's values are truly problematic, one cannot trade with it without being accused of hypocrisy.

Under Xi, the moment where these two stories are no longer fit for purpose has arrived. We now have no illusions about the business opportunities provided by China. It offers real but hard-won gains, with some investors such as Goldman Sachs and Apple winning big and others enduring spectacular failures – Mattel and Tesco, who both lost significant amounts of money and ended up closing their operations in China despite their initial success in the 2010s, spring to mind. In 2020, the Beijing government introduced the idea of 'dual circulation', a framework prioritising domestic consumption which would make Chinese citizens the source of future economic growth, rather than exporting goods to an increasingly fickle and unreliable outside world. Even so, China still stressed that it wanted to maintain good links with partners in tech and other areas where the country remained behind the West. Ironically, the Chinese population could provide clients for the sophisticated services sector in terms of insurance, different investment products and mortgages for their property that many Western companies dream of accessing – precisely at the time when, for political reasons, such an opportunity is harder to take advantage of due to antagonism with the country. The EU–China Comprehensive Agreement on Investment, for example, was negotiated for seven years;

although it was, perhaps, the first European deal with China where the EU came out on top by opening up the services sector in the People's Republic, the European Parliament overwhelmingly refused to ratify it in Spring 2021, because of sanctions that the Chinese government had deployed against five of its members.[16]

With regard to moral and political values, the situation is even more vexed. Xinjiang is a lamentable example, where since 2017 the establishment of 're-education camps' have seen the detention of an estimated 1 million people, largely of Uyghur ethnicity. The treatment of the Uyghurs shows Xi's China at its most disturbing. Parliaments of Western countries like Canada started to deploy the phrase 'genocide' as news of the crackdown in the region seeped to the wider world, although tellingly some other governments were less keen to follow their lead.[17] These disturbing developments sat alongside a devastating purge of dissidents and other contrarian domestic forces, beginning in 2015 when over 300 Chinese human rights lawyers were detained in one crackdown.[18] The consensus among well-informed observers, such as Reporters sans Frontières and Human Rights Watch, is that for academics, and for people working in the civil society sector, things are tougher than they have been for decades. The party has the most advanced surveillance technology in the world. This is not Mao's China. Then, technology was minimal, often ineffective, and the state maintained control through copious human surveillance – neighbours, colleagues at school, even family and friends. For Xi, artificial intelligence, facial recognition technology and mobile apps keeping tabs on people are important tools. This is, as the *Economist* has called it, digital totalitarianism at its most complete, the velvet prison par excellence.[19]

And yet, before one becomes too comfortably ensconced in the story of China as the human rights hell, there is the irrefutable fact that, materially, the vast majority of Chinese people have never been better off. A country that experienced mass famine in the early 1960s, which caused the deaths of possibly as many as 36 million people, has long since solved its food supply challenges. At the 2021 annual gathering of the country's parliament, the National People's Congress, the Chinese government declared that it had abolished 'absolute poverty' (defined in China as people living on less than $2.30 a day). Never before have more Chinese travelled abroad, with a staggering 169 million overseas trips taking place in 2019. More young people attend university, either domestically or outside the country, than at any point in the nation's history. The middle class have secured stronger property rights, and more opportunities at work and in education as well as in their daily lives. Their interests are looked after by officials who now, whether through fear, discipline or an actual sense of duty, are more likely to obey regulations in case they attract the interest of the dreaded anti-corruption body, the National Supervision Commission. Xi Jinping has also removed ambiguity in business and diplomacy, in a country where connections (the fabled *guanxi*), the back door and under-the-table deals used to be standard practice. Although the legal reforms brought in since 2013 have brought no succour to dissidents and those fighting for civil rights, commercially they have made things crystal clear. Courts that used to issue judgments that went largely ignored are now in the business of being heard. The lax implementation of rules was one of the prime complaints made by outsiders in the Hu era. Now, strangely, they complain of the opposite – far from making unfulfilled promises, the party does indeed carry out what it has said it would.

If one has a simplistic, monolithic view of China, then the power Xi possesses, and the sort of politician he is, will also seem similarly monolithic and straightforward. In this interpretation, he is the man who has removed all opposition, and who stands completely alone, like some colossus in the midst of a largely empty plain. Everything in this vast country comes to his attention and is subject to his decree. As Australian sinologist Geremie Barmé has put it, he is the Chairman of everything.[20] And yet over-fixation on this neat story fails to explain quite how it is that such a vast and complex country should become the fiefdom of one man. The

Communist Party that Xi leads today is 95 million members strong. In the 2021 census, the population edged over 1.4 billion people – China is a place that seems to have every shade of humanity. Never before has its population been so complex and hard to categorise. At least 5 million of them have been educated at degree level abroad. They are users of over 1 billion smart phones. China's civil service employs around 8 million people, with about ten times that number working for state enterprises. The vast majority of the rest of the working population are employed in businesses, or own different kinds of enterprises, many of which, on paper at least, are classified as non-governmental. In China's vast terrain, people are living every conceivable lifestyle, with the country going through a sexual revolution reminiscent of that experienced by Europe in the 1960s with rising levels of divorce, people living together before marrying, and engaging in extramarital affairs, only vaster in scale, and quicker. The Cultural Revolution of the 1960s ended in political failure once Mao died. Today's cultural revolution, an ongoing transformation where economic, social and technological change, and openness to the wider world, is reaching deep into the lives of every Chinese person in ways never seen before.

And yet, while the lives of the population become more complex, the story of the country's leadership and its politics mysteriously seems to have travelled in the opposite direction. Gone are the myriad factions and different parts of the Communist Party that figured in accounts from last century, when respected analysts like Cheng Li of the Brookings Institution could talk of the Shanghai, Princeling and Youth League factions in the party. Gone too is any sense of internal opposition. Even in the Mao era, when the costs of going against the Chairman were staggeringly high, there was always at least some form of dissent, voiced by people like his defence minister in the 1950s, Peng Dehuai, who was felled after criticising Mao following the famine in the early 1960s. In the Deng Xiaoping era, there were people such as Deng Liqun (no relative) who was deeply critical of the post-1978 reform process, which led to China engaging more with the outside world and taking on some capitalist practices. This group of dissidents were significant enough to merit their own label – the new Leftists. Jiang Zemin and Hu Jintao both had to deal with internal opponents. Apart from his tussle at the very start of his period in office with fellow Politburo member Bo Xilai, who was ultimately imprisoned, Xi seems to have faced nothing like this kind of depth and force of opposition. There have been some grumblings – an open letter published online, for instance, by an unnamed critic in 2015, or articles by businesspeople voicing unease at his style of rule. One individual from within the party, Cai Xia, did declare that Xi had become a dictator – but only after she left the party and had gone into exile to the US in 2020. For a leader who has even abolished time limits for being the country's president, as Xi did in 2018, it is a mystery as to why there has been so little internal opposition.

There is certainly a climate of fear in contemporary China. But the country has always had a history of courageous individuals who have spoken out no matter the cost, even during the Mao, Deng and Jiang years. Figures from that era such as Hu Feng in the 1950s, Li Yizhe from the 1970s,* Wei Jingsheng in the 1980s and 1990s and Liu Xiaobo in the 21st century all come to mind. Some of them languished in jail for years because of their opposition to the government. Why has there been so little of this under Xi, at a time when the opportunity to speak through the internet and other mediums has never been greater? I suspect this is a result of the power of the story the party is telling about China. The reality is that despite any issues the Chinese people might have about Xi, opposition to him inside and outside the party is made difficult by the fact that he and the party have bolted his style of leadership to the widely supported mission of making China a great, powerful country. This is not an abstract dream pushed into the distant future, as it was in the time of Mao, Deng, Jiang or Hu. Xi can realistically promise that on his watch, barring disaster, China will finally be said to have achieved modernity on its

---

* A pen name for three people working together – Li Zhengtian, Chen Yiyang and Wang Xizhe.

own terms, while maintaining political stability. The signs of this are everywhere. Under his stewardship, China has already set up a space station and landed spacecrafts on Mars. It has constructed more high-speed rail than the rest of the world put together – some 40,000 kilometres and counting. According to one international university ranking list, it has seen half a dozen of its universities enter the global top 50, with Beijing and Tsinghua universities edging into the top ten.[21] A country formerly accused of being an intellectual property thief is now, as shown in the revised 2020 partial trade deal with the Americans, keen on better protection because of its inventions and innovations in artificial intelligence, telecoms and life sciences. In terms of vessels, if not in technology, China has the world's largest navy. But the show is not remotely over. Sometime in the next decade, China will go to sleep one night as the world's second largest economy and wake up the next day as number one. Psychologically, symbolically and geopolitically, this will be a moment of enormous import. In some ways, it will change nothing: in per capita terms the country will still be far behind the US, European and many other countries. But it will also change everything: in terms of sheer economic size, for the first time since the Second World War, the US will no longer be top dog. The world's greatest capitalist will be a Communist-led country. This is not where history, as seen by supporters of liberal democracy, was meant to end.

With these prospects it is not hard to see why even those in China with reservations about Xi as an individual or his approach might find him a tricky figure to condemn openly. In the past, China's success was always contested. Its achievements under Xi can be questioned and re-contextualised, but there is no disputing the space landings, the high-speed trains, the inventions. They are real. They are happening. As long as projects like these are going in the right direction, contributing to the great objective of national rejuvenation so often stated in current propaganda, to dissent would be a sign of being a bad patriot – and Chinese people are, broadly, very patriotic. It may well be that the Xi leadership is manipulating and exploiting them. Indeed, it would be very incompetent not to do so. But the stereotype in much of today's Western discourse about China of the gullible, manipulated Chinese person, a target of state management and control, is just that – a stereotype. Xi's vision is effective, and he has proved a hard target for dissidents to dismiss not merely through the repression of any opposition, but for the rather more unpalatable fact that his style of politics, and the messages underlying it, appeals to the emotions and aspirations of many Chinese. His vision offers a positive image of their nation which, after a tough, often calamitous modern history, is finally emerging as a winner on the global stage. Maybe under the surface there is less support for the current leader of the Communist Party than one sees. Chinese people are probably no less nor more cynical about their leaders than people anywhere else. But if the largely unqualified, and politically inexperienced, Donald Trump could successfully run for the highest office in the US because many of his supporters thought him an idiot, but that he was their idiot, then why not apply the same logic to the reign of Xi?

In many ways, contrasting Xi with the forty-fifth President of the United States is helpful in understanding the Chinese leader. Unlike Trump, there is no shadow of doubt about Xi's commitment to the political force he heads and the need for its unity and cohesion. He enforces discipline and obedience. Nor can Xi be accused of being disdainful of intellectuals and experts. He peppers his speech with references to thinkers in ways that Trump never did. Ironically, with the commitment to the Paris Agreement on climate change as the main evidence, Xi is a far more committed globalist than Trump. When Trump's replacement, Joe Biden, took the US back into the Paris Agreement in 2021, China along with the US and many others signed up to the COP26 deal to ultimately phase out fossil fuels, though Xi didn't attend in person. As Xi's talk at the 2017 World Economic Forum at Davos set out, the paradox is not that China wants to make a completely new world order to replace the current one, but that it is increasingly committed to many of the current features of Western-originated globalisation in terms of participation in multilateral fora like the UN conventions, and entities like the World Trade Organization. This is probably because Xi understands, in a way Trump never bothered to, the integral links between individual nations and the sort of existential threats – from climate change to global pandemics – that face them, which cannot be solved without collective action. Under Xi, there is no argument about whether these issues should be taken seriously, nor of playing to domestic audiences by withdrawing from existing conventions. Unlike Trump, Xi is experienced in governance and public administration. His governments have largely been stable: in both his first and second standing committees of the Politburo, which is the equivalent of a top-level political cabinet in the Chinese system, no one who served was fired or removed from office. His administration's control over leaks has been unnerving, and complete. With Trump, by all accounts, the situation was the reverse. Trump's final management of the pandemic crisis – an event that contributed hugely to his defeat in the 2020 election – underlines the difference between the two men. Despite its savage impact, Covid-19 has only made Xi seem more entrenched and secure in his role. Trump lost power in his political system; at the moment, Xi continues to win in his. This is the ultimate benchmark of effective politics where home wins always matter more than those played away.

Seeing Xi Jinping principally as a politician, this book aims to examine in depth how his political power works. It will eschew easy binary views and the neat narrative of Xi as the all-powerful dictator. Instead, it will attempt to offer something more nuanced. When Xi took office in 2012, the seeming ease with which he managed to gain all the key levers of power intrigued me. Something seemed to be happening, although no one had noticed when it began. In fact, we were seeing the end of a process that had started long before. What sort of process was this, and what was it meant to achieve? In the 1990s, he was a provincial leader largely regarded as undistinguished and unlikely to gain national prominence. At the 1997 Party Congress, Xi received the lowest number of votes out of the 151 alternate members of the Central Committee, far from the centre of power.[22] To compound things, Xi's father was a high-ranking military and political figure in the Mao and Deng eras, at a time when politicians who were judged to be offspring of former party elites were highly unpopular. His future looked dim. There was no inevitability about his ascent to power. Behind the façade, in the opaque workings of the party, Xi must have had something that differentiated him from the many other contenders in the highly competitive and ruthless world of Chinese elite politics, one where the stakes have always been horribly high.

Only in the very final stages of Xi's journey to power, around mid-2007, did his selection for ultimate office become more obvious to observers. And the process by which the final decision was made to appoint him party boss and country leader in 2012 is still, to this day, shrouded in mystery. Clearly, Xi's individual qualities and convictions were crucial to his success and meant he ultimately emerged the winner over his competitors. But what were these qualities and convictions?

In hindsight, the views Xi had espoused in Zhejiang, earlier in his career, which are described in this book, can now be interpreted as a manifesto. They give insights into what made him tick back then, and therefore what sort of qualities and ideas he had that made him different from others. These garnered broader support far beyond his own individual appeal. In the thoughts he promoted in the years immediately before coming to Beijing to be a player in national politics, he forcefully supported a greater division between the worlds of politics and business. He had greater confidence, too, in speaking about China having a moral right to a higher status on the world stage. The deep belief in the country's destiny as a powerful, strong and rejuvenated nation was key, along with a desire to ensure the emerging middle class were better served in terms of property rights and public policy by a Communist Party which acted on principle, rather than solely to preserve the privileges and perks of its members. The absolute centrality of the party's mission to make China a great country again is evident from Xi's earliest recorded statements. This is surprising when one thinks of the general erosion of belief in the honesty and integrity of officials during the years of excess and material enrichment in the Hu period, when levels of corruption were so high. That pure, almost zealous, message was something that resonated with a significant number of the political elite, as well as members of wider Chinese society.

History is not necessarily shaped by the figures with the most ability, nor by the brightest, but by people with the strongest faith. Xi is a Communist leader in a country often accused of having no real beliefs, run by a system that only values having power as an end in itself. But this book will argue that, in fact, Xi is a man of faith, and that it was the quality and intensity of his faith that has taken him to where he is today. The greatest mistake the rest of the world makes about Xi is to not take this faith seriously. The hardship of his early years, his long period in the political wilderness outside of Beijing, his air of confidence and ambition despite the setbacks he experienced, are important evidence for seeing this faith in action. In post-Mao China, people often declared that Mao was man, not God. He had been misunderstood and miscategorised. Xi, too, is no divinity. But while he may subscribe to an atheist creed, for him, God is the Communist Party – and it is in demonstrating loyalty, commitment and total faith to that epic cause that his power, and his mission, have meaning. And as leader of a country that constitutes a fifth of humanity, which is set to have an impact on all the major questions of our collective future, whether we like the nature of Xi's faith or not, we have no choice but to take it seriously. To not do so would be a catastrophic mistake.

CHAPTER TWO

The Xi Story – 1953–2002

These days, the training centre for Communist Party offi-cials is spread between the Central Party School in the north-east of Beijing and what used to be called the School for Governance and Administration. In 2015, I was staying in the hotel in the School as part of an Australian government delegation sent to learn more about how China operated. I wandered around the calm and relaxing gardens, past the empty Olympic-sized swimming pool and through the restaurant. On the surface, it resembled any other convention centre. But the dense Chinese-language slogans in the reception area and the images on the LCD displays were a little more indicative of the true function of the buildings and what the usual visitors were there to do. The main inhabitants were those in the Chinese cadre system rather than us 'honorary residents'. 'Tell the China story,' they were instructed by these notices, almost ad nauseum. Back in my spartan room, I looked at the reading material left for the residents. A book sat at the front of the shelf entitled *Xi Jinping Stories*. In a break with precedent, a cartoon of the benignly smiling party secretary stared from the cover page. That a cartoonist who had rendered an image of Xi's predecessor, Hu Jintao, in a newspaper a few years earlier had received a prison sentence for disrespect showed how times had changed.

In the third decade of the 21st century China is in the era of storytelling. In 2017, the Party official newspaper, *The People's Daily*, produced a follow-up to the book mentioned above: *Xi Jinping Tells Stories*. Soon after his elevation as supreme office holder in the party and the state in 2013, Xi told his fellow Politburo members and the Ministry of Foreign Affairs that they needed to tell stories. By this he meant that they needed to do a better job of controlling how the narrative of their country was presented, and to combat the often negative images of China that were spread through the world – its human rights issues, its environmental problems, its social and economic inequality and the corruption of its officials. Xi insisted on 'objectivity' in these declarations – and of proactively telling people the many stories of China's success over the past few decades.

Xi's own story has been a key part of this exercise. His pathway in life serves as an analogy for the recent history of China – from his early years as the son of a privileged, high-ranking family in Beijing in the 1950s, to the disgrace of his father's house arrest in 1962, to the hardship he suffered after being exiled from Beijing in the latter part of that decade and the subsequent toil as he climbed back into social respectability and political success. Like that of the country itself, this is a tale of renaissance, prevailing over tough challenges and conditions and ending up in a place of vindication. Xi is the everyman of modern China in many ways – someone who persisted, learning each step of the way as he carried on his career, driven by an inner sense of mission and destiny. That, at least, is the official version.

Xi's immediate predecessor Hu Jintao was famously silent about his own autobiography. In his public declarations, and in official material about him, Hu was the man from nowhere. It was not known exactly where he had been born, when his parents had died or how he had managed to end up an elite leader after long years in provincial positions, such as in the south-western province of Guangxi, Gansu in the north and finally Tibet. Hu's oratory was robotic, driven largely by statistics, with a strong air of impersonality. Conversely, Xi used more emotional and personal language, with something of the pithiness and the willingness to speak in the first person that Mao Zedong had shown a fondness for. Almost from the moment he was announced as the top leader of the Communist Party in November 2012, the propaganda apparatus spoke a lot about Xi as a person – who he was, who his father had been, what he had done before becoming ultimate boss. They also spoke about his interests in literature, sport and other cultural matters. For a political environment in which the dominant attitude in recent decades had been to downplay the personal, and stress the collective, this in itself was a radical departure. Xi's story is part of the Xi political offer. The mode of its telling, the elements that are picked out for particular attention, and the ways these are used, are all important.

There are perfectly valid questions about how the story of Xi's pathway to power has been presented by him and the Communist Party he now heads, parts of which can be accepted as true, parts of which have been elaborated and adorned and, most frustratingly of course, parts of which have been conveniently forgotten or actively repressed. These issues hamper the efforts of scholars to write authoritative and complete accounts of figures such as Mao and Deng Xiaoping, for whom far more records exist, and for whom there is a greater understanding of their background and their subsequent career. The party guards secrets well. Those seeking to dig deeper into Xi's background, like the Bloomberg and *New York Times* reports which asked questions about his family and their wealth in 2011 and 2012, would not have been surprised by the sharp reprisals they received. Both *New York Times* and Bloomberg had their websites immediately blocked.

Despite this, the kind of story that is told of Xi, and the themes it encapsulates, tells us something important; it is indicative of the way that the party regards power, and what a politician should be doing. Many stories could have been told, some of which, as in the Hu era, would have downplayed the role of the central leader and of the institution of leadership. We now know that the choice was made, either by Xi or those in his closest network, to invest in a particular narrative – a Chinese political version of the 'hero tested by adverse circumstances'. Central to this is the period of seven years that Xi spent in his adolescence and early adulthood in Shaanxi province, at that time an undeveloped area that typified much about the poverty of rural China during the Mao era.

Xi was born in June 1953 in Beijing. His father, Xi Zhongxun, had been a military leader through the 1930s and 1940s, during the Sino-Japanese War, and then the Civil War from 1945 to 1949. He worked as deputy director of the Communist Party's organisation department (in charge of its personnel appointments) and then as a political commissar for the whole north-west of the country prior to 1949. For much of this time he was working in Yan'an. This was the place that Mao and the Communist Party had chosen as their remote base in 1936. A small settlement in the northern part of Shaanxi province, it was known for its primitive conditions, with local peasants living in caves, and its arid, tough agricultural climate. That Xi's son, Jinping, over two decades later and in utterly different circumstances, would be exiled there, a place with such deep emotional and symbolic meaning to the party, is important. It gives an extra layer of authenticity to Xi's current story. Like Mao, and the other elite leaders at the time of the party's greatest troubles, Xi Jinping himself also had his Yan'an time, in the very place where the party had established itself and, despite the most testing conditions, survived and finally prevailed.

Xi Zhongxun moved to Beijing when the new state was established in 1949. He was appointed to lead the party's propaganda department.* Elected as a member of the top-level leadership body of the Communist Party, the Central Committee, in 1956, he was further promoted in 1959 to become one of several vice-premiers working in the parallel government system of the State Council, the Chinese equivalent of the cabinet in the US or British system. All was going well. Xi Zhongxun had an important role in formulating policy and overseeing cultural issues. But unexpected dangers awaited in the turbulent period that began in the late 1950s. China broke with its most important ally and patron, the Soviet Union, in 1960, largely over the de-Stalinisation process that

---

* This was a party, rather than a state, function, something that remains the case today.

the country was implementing under Stalin's successor, Nikita Khrushchev. Mao's style of rule, which had initially been more collegial, became increasingly assertive and autocratic. The Great Leap Forward was introduced in 1958 to strengthen China's self-dependency, industrialisation and manufacturing but caused resources to be dramatically overstretched. Most devastating of all, in 1960, a combination of official mistakes and poor weather caused the country's harvests to fail. In the tragic famine that followed, between 20 and 50 million people starved to death, although it is impossible to know the true figure.[1]

In the midst of this, Mao became embroiled in a number of arguments with his colleagues, including Xi senior. Attracting the attention of Mao's feared security supremo, Kang Sheng, he was accused of having permitted the publication of a novel which was regarded as offering a critical view of Mao under the guise of a piece of fiction. Such use of indirect means to criticise real people in Chinese politics is a long-standing one, largely because of the high costs incurred by direct criticism. Xi senior was placed under investigation, stripped of his positions and put under house arrest. The impact of this on Xi Jinping, then nine years old, and his two brothers and two sisters was huge. Almost immediately, they went from being the cossetted offspring of a powerful central leader to a household with a deeply uncertain fate. The sole source of stability was

Qi Xin, their mother, who continued to work at the Central Party School (then called the Marx School of Communism).

There was more uncertainty to come when the Cultural Revolution started in May 1966. Mao Zedong's 'Great Cultural Proletariat Revolution' was one of the most complex, important events in modern Chinese history. It lasted for a decade in one guise or another and shaped the mindset of a generation. What began as a power struggle in Beijing between Mao and many of his long-term colleagues soon grew to become a vast attempt to remake society according to utopian ideals. The effects were highly unpredictable, and often violent. Schools and colleges closed. Students were encouraged to wage revolution by joining the Red Guards, revolutionary groups that were springing up across the country. People were labelled by class, meaning that those who were regarded as problematic because of their links to the Nationalist Party, which had opposed the Communist Party in the past, or who were classified as either landlords or intellectuals, or had links with them, often endured humiliation and denunciation. All too often, even far worse things happened, with hundreds of thousands of individuals tortured, wounded and in many cases murdered.

That Xi Zhongxun was judged a politically problematic case meant that Jinping and his siblings were in a vulnerable position from the start. For the first few years of the new revolution, however, their lives continued largely as normal, despite the rising uncertainty around them. But in December 1968, Mao Zedong issued one of his decisive, God-like edicts, commanding through an editorial in the party's mouthpiece, the *People's Daily* newspaper, that 'educated youth from the cities need to go to the countryside, to be re-educated by the farmers'. Almost immediately, a great wave of people similar to Xi – high school teenagers living in cities – had to uproot themselves and be assigned a new place to live in the countryside. Their schooling stopped and a wholly new life among complete strangers began. Xi remained in this rural exile for an unusually extended period. From the early 1970s, as the intensity and focus of the Cultural Revolution changed, many of the original 'sent-down youth' (as they came to be called) returned to their native cities, but Xi would not do so until 1975. By that time, he had finally, after nine previous attempts, succeeded in joining the Communist Party, despite the massive shadow that hung over his father (who remained under house arrest until after Mao Zedong's death in 1976) and had become the leader of a small commune – the first of his official positions.

Xi's time in rural Yan'an is presented in contemporary Chinese propaganda as providing signs of his authentic links to the countryside. He is a peasant emperor – a phrase which was used, perhaps with more conviction, about Mao. Unlike previous leaders whose careers and lives were rooted in more urban contexts, Xi's depth and breadth of lived experience in rural China is posited as being unique and important. This was the era during which, by some accounts, he worked as a pig farmer and, by others, lived in a cave.

The testimonies of those who were sent down with Xi from Beijing give a better image of what life was like. Aged barely fifteen, he was among the youngest of the cohort. In early January 1969, just a few weeks after the Mao command was given, Xi and around twenty other students were put on a train from Beijing to the Yan'an area. Yan'an itself is a prefecture, the third of five levels of governmental administration in modern China – national, provincial, prefectural, county and town. That meant it covered a huge area, containing ten counties, two districts and a city. Once Xi arrived in the main city of Zichang, he was transferred to Yanchuan district in the eastern part of the prefecture. But his journey was not over. He and about ten other youths were taken by bus for several hours along increasingly primitive roads from the county town to the village of Liangjiahe.

Contemporaries paint a mixed picture of Xi's new home.[2] Subsequent research on the sent-down youth presents a pattern of callow, sometimes idealistic and frequently untested young people being sent into communities that regarded them as burdens. In some cases, students were bullied and exploited.

There are records of young women being abused and raped. Even in the more benign environment of Xi's village, the new cohort of arrivals were a strain on local resources – from the allocation of food to their accommodation. They also needed proper agricultural training to be useful. One of Xi's peers talked of arriving after their long journey and spending their first night far from home sleeping on stone platforms called *kangs*, one for women, one for men. It was bitterly cold. But worse than this was the large number of bugs and insects that infested the sleeping area. The food was unfamiliar and wholly different to their diets in Beijing. Shaanxi food was more based on fatty pork and different kinds of vegetables. Each morning people were expected to rise literally with the calling of the cockerel, something that might happen around 3 or 4am.[3]

The work was soul destroying and back-breaking – digging and preparing farmland, harvesting crops and tending animals. On top of this, there was an inevitable cultural and social divide between the youth and the villagers. Despite the aims of the revolution to create an egalitarian society, the fact was that two decades after the Communists had come to power, a place like Liangjiahe lacked such basic amenities as hot running water, sanitation and the provision of electric or gas power. Ironically, it was Xi's efforts to address the energy issue when he became a local party official in 1974 that set him out, in the eyes of locals, as an effective leader and champion of their cause. For city people, Liangjiahe was like another planet, where the locals spoke a different dialect, had a highly insular mindset and were largely consumed by their need to simply survive in a harsh environment with very limited assets. For Xi, as for the future leader Deng Xiaoping and the well-known dissident Wei Jingsheng, both of whom were exiled at a similar time to Xi (with the latter taking part in the same sent-down movement), the question was simple: how exactly has the Communist revolution made any material difference to the living standards of ordinary Chinese people – the very people whose efforts had brought the party to power? The answer was not obvious.

What impression did Xi make on those who were sent to Liangjiahe with him? He was regarded as bookish, bringing a heavy satchel of works with him from Beijing. He is said to have read Carl von Clausewitz's *On War* while in the village, as well as an early book by Henry Kissinger. He had a particular interest in modern history and the Chinese classics. He used a light to read deep into the night, while others, exhausted, slept nearby, ready for the next day of hard labour. Xi was regarded as polite, with a sense of purpose, but someone who did not speak a huge amount unless he had to. It seems he made a decent impression on the farmers, who were largely unaware of his famous father and, therefore, of the complexities of his background.

When Xi first attempted to join the party around 1973, he was seen as being problematic by the local party apparatus. He had a good work record, an excellent attitude and evident loyalty to the party. The problem was his family background, and the fact that his father remained incarcerated, spending time either under house arrest, or in prison. During the instability of the Cultural Revolution, allowing the son of a disgraced leader like Xi Zhongxun to join the party was the type of sign of disloyalty that more zealous leaders might target, and hold local cadres accountable for. Xi certainly had the support of the officials in his village, and the brigades around it. The problem was that a key person in the local township refused to budge, rejecting Xi's attempts to join a number of times. Their removal to another post in late 1973 meant that Xi was finally allowed to join in 1974, which, in turn, meant that he could then be appointed to local administrative positions. He then became the party boss of the small village, with the consent of the villagers. The party seems to have forgotten its initial chariness quickly, and local papers applauded him as a model party worker in 1974 and 1975.[4]

It is hard to assess the accuracy of the reports that exist about Xi's brief period as a village official. Much of this information has been framed by what happened afterwards, as though it inevitably prefigured the great events that happened decades in the future. Xi is shown as being someone utterly focussed on the needs of the local people, someone who was keen on actions rather than words, and who did not mind getting involved in the most basic tasks. By this account, he sounds like the model figures in Chinese Communist lore like 'Iron Man' Wang Jinxi or Lei Feng of a decade before. These were selfless individuals whose lives were wholly committed to the good of the party, and who figured in subsequent propaganda to mobilise and incentivise the Chinese people. The Xi myth has an element of this archetype, painting him as a diligent party leader, one who resisted arrogance, corruption and incompetence. Interestingly, in 1998, Xi himself wrote of his initial life in Shaanxi in far more negative terms in an autobiographical fragment, 'Son of the Yellow Earth'. The fleas, dirt and poverty hugely affected him. 'When I first came to the Yellow Earth as a fifteen-year-old, I was perplexed and lost,' he explained. 'I was compelled by circumstances to go to the countryside when I was very young. I did not pay attention to the issue of unity because I did not plan to stay for long. Every day, others went to work in the mountains but I was very casual about work. The folks did not make a good impression on me. I went back to Beijing after a few months and was then sent to the old revolutionary base in Taihang Mountain.'[5] Even in this more subdued account, however, the moral message Xi drew from his experiences was clear: 'When I left at 22, I had firmly established my life's purpose and was full of confidence.

As a servant of the people, my root is in the plateau of northern Shaanxi. For it planted a firm belief in me: to do practical things for the people.' The experience, in his own words, 'built up my self-confidence. As the saying goes, *the knife is sharpened on a grinding stone and a man is made through hardships.*'[6]

In 1975, with a call for people to attend the recently reopened universities and colleges, Xi successfully applied to study engineering at the elite Beijing Tsinghua University. He left the village but maintained contact with the villagers over the coming decades. Village leaders went to see him when he attained higher office in Fujian province in the 1990s. They also tracked him down in the 2000s when he had moved on to Zhejiang. Each time, according to the official account at least, Xi helped them with their problems. Finally, as leader of the country in the 2010s, he returned to the place he had lived for seven years, which, in many ways, supplied his core political education, and was given an almost regal reception by those who remembered his life there decades before.

When Xi rose to ultimate power, former Singaporean leader Lee Kuan Yew was prompted to say that he was 'Asia's Mandela', because of the hardship he had suffered during his Liangjiahe years.[7] The truth, even from the scant records that are available today, is a little more nuanced. Despite the hardship, in many ways, Xi ended up having a relatively unproblematic Cultural Revolution. He managed to survive the stigma of being his father's son, became a party member and gained experience which, in practical and symbolic terms, has subsequently given him rich returns. Nor is there any evidence he was involved in some of the more violent actions that took place then, claims of which have come back to haunt certain former colleagues of his such as Bo Xilai, a competitor in the 2000s, who was accused of beating his own father during this period to prove his radical status. Xi was dealt a difficult hand over this period – as were many others – but not a wholly terrible one. His greatest achievement was that he survived. Many others at this time didn't, including, tragically, his half-sister from his father's first marriage, Heping, who reportedly ended her life in the early 1970s because of the suffering she had endured. It is also striking that for all the claims made by others about his sent-down years, Xi himself has referred to this time only rarely, and almost always with criticism. He does not seem remotely nostalgic about the Shaanxi years, as his autobiography of 1998 shows. 'Later in life, whenever I ran into difficulties,' he wrote, 'I would think of that period. How could I not carry on now when I could work under those extremely difficult conditions? The difficulties now are no comparison to the difficulties then.'[8]

After three years' study at university, Xi's family circumstances changed. A photo from around 1977 shows him as a young man, walking behind his father who had recently been freed from house arrest. Xi senior was one of the many whose cases were reviewed once Mao had died and the Cultural Revolution ended; he was quickly restored to important positions, the most historically significant of which was as party first secretary in Guangdong province where he served from 1979 into the 1980s. Xi junior initially worked in the military, serving as the assistant to Geng Biao, a major People's Liberation Army leader. The Xis had rejoined the political elite. Had he continued in this sector, perhaps today he would be the head of the Chinese army, navy or air force. But in another of those crucial moments in his life path, around 1982, Xi decided to transfer to the civilian side of governance. He moved to Zhending county, in Hebei province, about 240 kilometres south of Beijing. From there, in 1985, he would move to Fujian, the huge, dynamic coastal province facing Taiwan in the south-east of the country, which would serve as his home until 2002.

The year 1982 marked another change in Xi's life: it was also the year his brief first marriage to Ke Lingling ended, only three years after they had eloped together while in Beijing. Ke was the daughter of a senior diplomat, Ke Hua, who was sent to be ambassador to Britain in 1978, where he played a crucial role in the early negotiations for the return of Hong Kong. The couple's marriage failed because Ke had followed her father to Britain. Ke Hua died in 2019 at the age of 103 but, according to rumour, she remains in London, a somewhat shadowy figure who has been linked to Huawei and Imperial College.

Xi's second wife was also a member of the elite, one of the most popular singers from the 1980s, Peng Liyuan, whom he married in 1987. Peng came from a family in Shandong. Under the patronage of powerful backers, she entered the People's Liberation Army. Clips of her regaling the loyal soldiers who repressed the 1989 Tiananmen Square uprising are still easily available online – although not, of course, from within China. Until the late 2000s, Peng was far more famous than her husband, pursuing her career in Beijing while he remained in Fujian in the south, working his way up the ranks. Chinese marriages at this level of political life are often treated almost as business deals. And yet the position of the person closest to the key leader is not without political influence, at least insofar as Peng has access to Xi in ways no one else does. Mao's fourth wife, the formidable Jiang Qing, became an infamously radical political demagogue in the last decade of the Chairman's time in power. Once he died, however, all vestiges of her influence vanished. Perhaps because of that unfortunate precedent, since then, political wives have remained in their husbands' shade, their influence largely unknown.* Peng has broken this model, taking formal positions for

---

* Since 1949, all members of the Standing Committee of the Politburo, the summit of power in modern China, have been men.

the United Nations and other bodies and speaking abroad; her English is good, unlike that of her husband. The couple's daughter, Xi Mingze, was born in 1992. Her father was apparently not at her birth because he was busy working. She went on to study at Harvard and, since her graduation and return to China, has sometimes served as a translator for her father.

Moving to Fujian in 1985 meant that Xi was in one of the most dynamic, trade-orientated places in China at exactly the same time as the economic experimentation, recently sanctioned by the central government, was starting to bear fruit. Xi's father, Zhongxun, while holding a senior position in Guangzhou, a neighbouring province, had been instrumental in bringing about these reforms, supporting the establishment of special economic zones licensed to make manufactured goods for export markets. Hong Kong and Taiwanese hi-tech and manufacturing companies took advantage of the plentiful land, tax breaks, favourable access to loans and almost unlimited cheap labour to move their plants into the People's Republic. For Fujian, with ports like that in the city of Xiamen facing Taiwan, the synergies were natural. Soon, large numbers of Taiwanese were working in the province, particularly from 1992 when a new wave of liberalisation and more reciprocal support from the Taiwanese government started.

Over this period, Xi witnessed reforms on the ground, and the impact they had on people's daily lives. The major city of Fuzhou, capital of Fujian province, where he worked much of the time before moving to the coastal port of Xiamen, was symptomatic of many of the other main urban centres in China. On a visit there in 1998, around the time Xi was based in the city, I remember the new airports, roads and skyscrapers that filled the metropolis, and the sense that most of the people living and working there had moved in from the surrounding countryside. Motorways took me further south, into one of the supposedly rural areas. But what was impressive was that even here the houses looked new and prosperous, and there was an air of almost tangible energy and entrepreneurial zeal. Xi no doubt saw the downsides of this rampant growth: rising inequality, the obvious signs of environmental degradation through the breakneck speed of industrialisation and, within the party at least, the deadly issues of corruption and malfeasance. Lai Changxing was the most famous example of this, a businessman who through his infamous 'red mansion', the villa that contained his headquarters, built up a network of corrupt officials induced through backhanders, sex and other temptations to support a vast smuggling ring. Billions of dollars were filtered away, with reports of Mercedes cars stuffed with cash being landed underwater on the Fujian coast, completely bypassing the customs officials. Lai seemed to have had his tentacles in every area of the province, running it like a shadow administration. In a clampdown in the late 1990s, however, his luck ran out. He fled to Canada, but after a long court case he was extradited back to China in 2011, where he was sentenced to life imprisonment.

Despite the many names that figured in the Lai network, Xi's was not one of them. That may have been luck, or maybe it was because the future leader was careful to steer clear of the offers made by Lai and his agents. In any case, it meant that Xi was one of the few senior local officials who emerged from the turmoil of this vast case largely untouched. However, corruption was not the only issue facing the province's governance. In the 1990s, Fujian gained a reputation as a major location for human trafficking. The majority of illegal Chinese arrivals in the UK in the late part of the decade were from Fujian, something that seemed puzzling because of the high levels of growth and prosperity the area was starting to experience. Why, when there were good opportunities for quick enrichment back home, would people still take the risk of attempting to move abroad to try their luck elsewhere? The consensus was that an initial taste of a different life only made some keener to try to experience something even better. The tragic incident in 2000 where 60 Chinese people – many of whom were from the Fujian area – were found hidden in a Dutch lorry embarking at the port of Dover, 58 of them already dead, all of them seeking a happier life than they believed they had in China and willing to take such huge risks, underlined just how deadly this issue could prove.

In the interviews that Xi gave over this period, one theme recurs – the need to maintain the boundaries between the political and business worlds. As an outsider, he was not surrounded by family members living locally who expected favourable treatment. This was a constant issue for officials who were working in their home territory, and the main reason why historically, even before the Communists came to power, the principal leaders of provincial areas appointed from the centre were almost always outsiders. Even so, the sheer speed of growth in the two decades since 1980 created perpetual imbalances, where everyone seemed to be able to 'jump into the sea', a phrase used about going into business. For Fujian, this was amplified by the fact that the area had a large number of foreign enterprises. There were money-making opportunities everywhere, either through people acting as intermediaries, suppliers, wholesalers or setting up small shops and businesses. Construction was booming and money was plentiful. Officials with the power to decide where, and when, to approve major projects were frequently subject to persuasive approaches. All of this happened while wages and conditions for public officials remained modest.

Quite why Xi took such a purist position is unclear. But it was something that remained with him on his move to the equally entrepreneurial coastal province of Zhejiang in 2002. There are rumours that his mother, the steely Qi Xin, summoned the family at some point in the 2000s and ordered them to keep firm boundaries between their private interests and public lives. But perhaps it was the looming influence of Xi's father. In the 1970s, during his years in the countryside, Xi junior had worked hard to prove to the people in his village that he could be a worthy party member and a good cadre, despite having what was then considered a controversial family background. Xi Zhongxun's rehabilitation in the late 1970s removed this stain, but only temporarily: on retirement in the late 1980s, he seemed to grow irritated with the party elite, reportedly exploding in rage at the hard-line Premier Li Peng at a meeting in 1990 for mismanaging the government response to the Tiananmen Square protests the year before. From this time, he lived in Shenzhen, and was never based in the capital again. Events like this may have instilled in his son, pursuing his own political career at the time, a sense of insecurity and a need to prove that his own party loyalty was rock solid. Zhongxun died in 2002, at the end of Xi's Fujian years.[9]

Fujian gave Xi plenty of experience, at county, prefecture and finally provincial levels of government. He served as governor of the whole area, the most senior administrative position, for his final two years. Over this period, remarkably, he was also able to complete a doctorate at his alma mater, Tsinghua University, in the area of Marxist legal theory. Questions remain about precisely how an extremely busy leader was able to allocate enough time to undertake study like this in only four years. That a former Fuzhou colleague, Chen Xi, had by that time become a senior leader in the university, ultimately becoming its party boss from 2002, only spiked the curiosity of observers further. The doctorate has been published online in Chinese and is a work of dense analysis, and firm Marxist orthodoxy. All one can conclude from this is that however Xi gained his degree, he obviously felt it was important to display an aptitude to learn.

Another facet of the Fujian years that was to bear fruit in Xi's future was the opportunity it gave him to engage with Taiwanese and other international businesses and to be exposed to the outside world. We don't know if Xi accompanied Geng Biao, his first boss in the army, when Geng went to the US in 1981. But certainly, soon after his arrival in Fujian, Xi went as part of a mission to visit Iowa in 1985. Much has been made of this, with some claiming that he 'studied' or 'lived' in America. In fact, he spent only a fortnight there. Even so, he resided in a typical house as a guest for a part of that time, revisiting it in 2015 on a state visit and recalling pleasant memories of his time there. Xi took part in other overseas trips throughout his time both in Fujian, and afterwards. This was all good preparation for the mammoth series of global travels he undertook from 2012 as leader – over 65 countries visited up to 2020, the most by any single leader of China.

Xi's transition to Zhejiang was a major promotion. In his five years there, he served as the party secretary, the most powerful political position in the province. It is to this period that we now turn.

CHAPTER THREE

The Zhejiang Years – 2002–2007

In 2001, while I was working in the British embassy in Beijing, one of my embassy duties was to accompany a British dignitary on a trade tour across China. After the obligatory brief stay in the capital to set the scene and meet senior leaders, we went off to Xi'an. Despite its fame as the home of the Terracotta Army, the city was not well developed. The centre was often chaotic, and the hotel service sometimes basic to non-existent. Even a two-day stay here left the less acclimatised British visitors a little frazzled. Perhaps that was why, when their plane landed at the next destination, Hangzhou, capital of the coastal Zhejiang province, they cheered up. The roads looked more modern. The hotels appeared neater and more orderly. There were functioning Science Parks and business zones that looked like they were actually producing innovative material, rather than merely saying they intended to. Zhejiang was an up-and-coming place, with some of the highest per capita GDP levels in the country. A year after our tour, the top leadership spot in this area went to Xi, fresh from his time in Fujian. In hindsight, the Zhejiang years proved crucial for his progress towards Beijing.

Chinese politicians are not like politicians in the West. This difference is about more than the fact that they will never be put forward for a public election. It is more about the long training and the very structured career on which they embark once they enter the political system. This may involve lengthy sojourns in more remote and less developed provinces. Xi's predecessor, the enigmatic Hu Jintao, had spent many years outside of Beijing in relatively undeveloped areas: Gansu province in the far north, then Guangxi and finally Tibet. Tibet was consumed by protests during Hu's time there in the late 1980s. The ability to deal with dissent in ways that please Beijing is one of the means of getting noticed by important patrons and finding one's way into the super elite. Hu's effective management of the 1987 and 1989 Lhasa unrest was one of the reasons given to his elevation as Jiang Zemin's successor.

It is well known that cadres go through exhaustive assessment procedures. In the past, regardless of the county, prefecture or other larger administrative area they oversaw, the principal aims were to ensure good economic growth and that there were no outbreaks of protests and instability. As time has gone on, however, more complex criteria have come to be applied. The ability to address environmental issues, for instance, or to improve wellbeing, social contentment and loyalty towards the party ideology and leadership.

The world of high-level officials in contemporary China is a very strange one. As Rowan Callick pointed out in his 2013 book on the Communist Party, *Party Time*, once you enter the highest levels of leadership your world changes. Distance opens up between you and the public. Your environment becomes one of leadership compounds, limousines carrying you from meeting to meeting, where bodyguards and minders make sure that you are kept away from any stray member of wider society who has not been vetted and approved for access.[1] There is a very good reason for this. To this day, China is a place where huge amounts of responsibility and power lie in the hands of relatively few people. Those with the greatest powers over resources, budget allocations and appointments of personnel are members of a tiny cohort. Of a population of 1.4 billion, the senior leadership of the Communist Party who might fall into this category are probably no more than 3,000 people.[2] Within their number lie a few super power-holders – significant figures in the Politburo, or the finance or security apparatus, whose decisions can make or break whole areas and communities. It would be a sobering exercise to find out who, in the end, was responsible for the widespread clampdown on over a million people in Xinjiang that began in 2017.

It is likely that the details were ultimately decided by no more than three or four people. And only one – Xi himself – would have given the final mandate.

Officials with this much power are the target of many who desire help from them, who have petitions they wish to present to them or those who have grown resentful about perceived injustices. The latter actively harbour malign intent towards the individuals they blame for these. Since 2012, occasional rumours have cropped up about Xi needing to sleep in a different place each night and surviving assassination attempts. True or not, they indicate the intense and constant pressure these figures are under. High-level officials speak of serving, and of being close to the people. But to an outside observer, top-level Chinese politicians look dangerously like a class apart.

Xi joined this elite group in 2002 when he became party secretary in Zhejiang. His life as a provincial governor in Fujian had been a little lower down the ladder. Xi gained this new position according to the various criterion of assessment set out above. But there would also have been something beyond this – because the number of competent and capable officials in China is still far higher than the high-level positions available for them. Lobbying, creating and then maintaining supportive enabling networks and seeking patronage in the centre also played a role. In this respect, Xi's links with figures like his former boss, Geng Biao, a major military leader for many years, who died at the age of 90 in 2000, were important. Even so, in 2002, Xi still had everything to prove. His time in Zhejiang was part of the long testing process that all officials at this level have to prove themselves in before moving to the next stage.

Zhejiang, one of China's 31 provinces and autonomous regions, wraps around Shanghai, the economic and logistic powerhouse of the country – indeed, of the whole of Asia. By the time Xi arrived there, it had already gained a reputation as a place of great entrepreneurialism. The most famous example of this was the Wenzhou area, which had been a relatively deprived, backward region but, despite this, became symbolic in China of the reforms that began in 1978, after the death of Mao. Wenzhou businesses and entrepreneurs had gone out in the world, setting up companies, sales support networks and other international business links in places as far afield as Prato in Italy and the west coast of the US where they dealt with imports and exports and textile production. The Wenzhou phenomenon came to be studied by economists in the 1980s and 1990s, who drew up various theories about how poor opportunities in the area meant that people went to seek new challenges elsewhere as soon as they were given the chance. Zhejiang had other great attributes. In the city of Hangzhou, it had a major university hub. The province also had train, road and water links to Beijing and Shanghai, as well as down the coast to Guangdong and Hong Kong. While Wenzhou was a deprived era, much of the rest of Zhejiang was historically prosperous because of its agriculture, silk industry and tourism assets. All of these figured in Xi's speeches and writings once he came to the area.

His predecessor, Zhang Dejiang, who had been in office since 1998, had managed to square the circle, encouraging the dynamic private enterprises springing up in Zhejiang to develop, find markets and grow, even as he asserted that they should not be allowed to be party members and that state control was the only legitimate way to run an economy. The ability to do one thing while saying another was permitted because in the only area that mattered – economic results – Zhejiang was a runaway success. From the mid-1990s until 2000, the GDP growth rate of the region was 10 per cent, placing it tenth among the 31 provinces and autonomous regions of the country. But from 2000 to 2005 it rocketed to 14.5 per cent, putting it second.[3] Concentrations of hi-tech start-up companies located in the region were part of the reason for this, including Alibaba, which was established in April 1999. A famous video exists from around that time of Alibaba's young founder, Jack Ma Yun, pitching to potential supporters in a small apartment in Hangzhou.[4] Within two decades of founding his start-up, the entrepreneur (who had once been an English teacher, and was even turned down for a job at Kentucky Fried Chicken), had turned his company into one of the most successful businesses not only in China but in the whole world. In the process, he became China's richest man.*

Xi was regarded as being relatively business-friendly in the city, not just to Chinese enterprises, but also to foreign ones. He was also someone who regularly penned short articles to communicate his ideas to a wider audience. These were published in a single volume, towards the end of his time in the province. *New Sayings from Zhejiang* gives an insight into his priorities and preoccupations during the Zhejiang years, and at a crucial time on his journey to national elite leadership in Beijing.

Reading through Xi's Zhejiang collection of articles, which has never been fully translated into English, a number of core themes emerge. These revolve around the centrality of the party and the need to have loyal, disciplined party officials and members; the imperative for stability and balanced growth and development; and the emerging issue of environmentalism. These ideas could be said to be the bedrock of Xi's belief system and have figured more strongly as he became a national leader. The first of these themes started to appear in Xi's words early in 2003. In June that year, he wrote of the need for officials to go 'deep in the masses of the people', to

---

* This, however, did not stop him falling under political suspicion in late 2020, because of critical comments he made about Chinese state banks, and briefly disappearing for three months.

unite with farmers, workers, intellectuals and all other social forces, in order to 'realistically hear their opinions, do things efficiently, in a detailed way, and according to regulations'. A few days later, he returned to this issue, wondering why it was that cadres 'were going into business', and complaining about them using their official platforms for making money. 'To be an official,' he declared, 'you need to have the moral standing of an official – and that means not always thinking of your-self.' A good cadre, he stated, 'can be recognised by people no matter what their level is. Your constant thought needs to be, what can I do for the party. What will my legacy be? You have to "use your power for the people".' Power is only useful 'if it is for the people', he wrote on 17 July that year. One had to 'cultivate deep feelings for the masses'. Somewhat startlingly, he referred back to the 1960s model citizen, Lei Feng, whose selfless devotion was part of the party mythology. Cadres had to 'manage themselves' and have 'morals and ability' – not devotion to some abstract ideological theories.

What were leading cadres with aspirations for leader-ship meant to do? What were their key tasks? According to Xi, they had to differentiate themselves from businesspeople or intellectuals. But how should they do this? In November 2003, he explained that they 'needed to stand on a vantage point and look around them across all of society', seeing things in the totality. In addition, they needed to be 'comprehensive, ambitious' and have 'an international perspective'. A metaphor he used a few days later made his point more clearly: officials were like the conductor of an orchestra. If they stopped their work, everyone would drift off into their own tune and unity would be lost. But his demands on cadres went deeper. They needed to do their work with feeling, not merely go through the motions. They needed to act with conviction, as though they actually believed in what they were doing and in the larger mission of their work. Above all, they could not procrastinate, or pay lip service to the task at hand. It was imperative they have faith. This was cast in a personal tone on 15 January 2004: 'The time one has as a leader is limited. You have to always ask yourself, why did I join the party, why did I want to be an official, what did I want to do, and what will my legacy be?' Xi persistently returns to phrases around 'using the party for public good' over this era, and a plea for officials to be realistic and task-orientated in their work. If they wanted to be any good, they had to 'take care of small things', and display party spirit. This differentiates them from corrupt cadres 'who only care about big things' and make empty promises. Arrogance and self-satisfaction were the enemies of the party. 'Some officials,' Xi stated on 6 April 2004, 'feel that if their mouths have spoken, and their meetings have been held, then that is all that matters.' There were other leading cadres who only wanted to say good things to those under them and never hold them to their word or demand accountability. Sure, they were nice guys, everyone liked them. But what, Xi demanded, did they end up actually doing except continuing the sense of self-interest, complacency and self-regard?

'Now, compared to the past, leading cadres have good work conditions. These are better than ever,' Xi declared on 12 May 2004. 'They have more powers than ever – but they should never think that this power is some kind of personal possession. It is for the people.' Leading cadres, he went on a few days later, 'should welcome being tested and disciplined by public opinion. They shouldn't peddle falsehoods or get involved in wasteful public events and pointless campaigns. The best leaders see hardships as an opportunity.' 'How should we deal with rising pressures,' he asked on 14 June, 'and expectations towards cadres? Some see the hardships as nothing more than a problem. But the really bold see these as an opportunity.' Cadres in the face of troubles should 'preserve a good bearing'. 'Dealing with contradictions and troubles is our basic work,' he said on 16 June. One had to be optimistic, no matter what fate threw at you. 'With no hardship and problems, then what jobs do cadres actually have?' Dealing with difficult issues is fundamental to their work; they should stop complaining and view this as a privilege.

Perhaps the most striking aspect of Xi's thinking on party matters over this era was the stress he put on moral standing.

At a time when the public were becoming increasingly cynical towards how officials used their powers, Xi demanded that 'to have ability, cadres have to have high morals. Without decent morals or good cultivation of high culture, even if you have great knowledge and ability, you won't be able to do great things.' The cancer of corruption and the threat it posed figured a week later on 26 July: 'The party needs to discipline and regulate itself much better and more seriously.' Some cadres 'just want to be good mates' to everyone. They practised a clubby 'you're OK, I'm OK' ethos, avoiding embracing criticism and opening themselves to evaluation. On the thorny issue of dealing with petitions submitted by disgruntled members of the public, Xi was also categorical. These complaints needed to be listened to and taken seriously. In their private lives, even when they were alone and no one was watching, officials from the top down needed to manage themselves and ensure they acted properly. They needed to be exemplary and behave as role models for everyone else.

With entry into the World Trade Organization in 2001, against the more pessimistic assessments of internal and external analysts, China moved into a period of rapid economic growth on an unprecedented scale. Double digit growth, as in Zhejiang, was the norm during this period. The party was, in many ways, becoming a casualty of its own success. Everyone was on the make. Business and money were the new objects of worship. But as deeply unwanted collateral from this, daily reports of staggering amounts of official malfeasance and corruption spread through new social media platforms. The confluence of galloping wealth creation and a whole new form of public scrutiny via the internet led to a series of embarrassing exposés. This situation only escalated as the decade wore on. One website contained pictures of the luxury watches worn by a single official in the undeveloped Shaanxi province; one of these alone would have cost several times his annual wage.[5] In another case, a mid-ranking official had accrued eleven mistresses – he was exposed when the mistresses ganged up and publicly denounced him.[6] Rumours of daily avalanches of wealth being siphoned off abroad were rife. The state sector looked like it was in danger of becoming similar to the fiefdoms of oligarchs who had risen in Russia after the collapse of the USSR in the 1990s. The party seemed to be losing influence and, even more devastatingly, power. It had become a tool for a self-serving network of officials, busy feathering their own nests.

This gives Xi's persistent imprecations over this period a particular edge. They often sound like sermons delivered by a priest trying to preserve the moral mandate of their church rather than statements by a politician defending their political party. Leading cadres, after all, the subject of so much of Xi's righteous ire, were crucial. They were, he said on 15 November

2004, 'the basis of all action for the party'. Their political consciousness mattered. So too did their moral quality, not merely their intellectual and administrative abilities. They needed to know that their first responsibility was to the organisation they belonged to and worked for, a responsibility that had remained unchanged since the time of the founding father Mao: to serve the people. The grass roots of the party was particularly crucial; it was where the contribution of officials was most visible, and where party and society worked indivisibly beside each other. 'Our party,' Xi stated on 23 January 2005, 'is the one in the world that most observes rank and hierarchy.' This ordering of ranks for officials means the party can be ordered, stable, with the top guiding everyone beneath, right down to the very bottom. If anywhere along this great chain of party existence, one official were rotten or incompetent, the whole edifice was threatened. It needed to be like a well-defended fortress. Cadres had to respect themselves and guard against arrogance. They had to convert pressure and challenges into motivation and opportunity. They had to constantly improve themselves and teach themselves. 'People,' Xi said on 7 February that year, 'need to look not just at how cadres speak, but what they do.'

For all their dynamism and enrichment, the 2000s were also a period of rising social tensions and deepening inequality. Mass incidents, defined as an event involving more than twenty people protesting at any one time over the same issue, were occurring almost daily across the whole country. Xi constantly referred to the 'scientific development' theory of the national party leader Hu, an unusually obedient stance for a provincial-level official at the time. Under this theory, the onus was on sustainability, balanced growth and harmony. And yet, China seemed anything but harmonious, with often large-scale explosions of anger erupting across the country. Some of these, as Yu Jianrong, an eminent Beijing-based social scientist, explained later in the decade, were from what he called 'righteous anger', over unaddressed abuses and injustices. Other protests were seen as opportunism and 'hooliganism'. The worst were instigated by what the party leadership regarded as its internal enemies, often supported by external backers, like the US, or human rights groups. These struck at the heart of the legitimacy of the party. In the mid-2000s, around the time of the colour revolutions in the former Soviet Union satellite states, where countries experienced protest and political change over frustrations related to corruption and repression, party analysts saw how easily civil society could morph into political opposition, led by lawyers and journalists championing human rights and freedom of speech. Under Hu, vast resources were put into 'pro-stability' policies, which damped down forces of opposition and antagonism. This was done by negotiation and discussion or, more usually, use of full-scale violence, as was the case in Dongzhou,

Guangdong province in 2005, where police quelled protestors with gunfire.[7] The requisition of land from farmers to be used in commercial development to supply a source of funds for local officials was a particular cause of huge disruption. Xi, as any other high-ranking provincial official at this time, was well aware of this problem, stating in December 2005 that 'the prime need is for stability. As people become wealthier, there is also the chance that they will become more divided and unstable.' These words were prescient; once Xi himself was sitting in the number one job after Hu's retirement, he would engage in even more difficult negotiations with different social groups about the kinds of contributions they needed to make to the new, rising China.

One way for the party to manage the deepening rift with other members of society was through better communication. In this respect, Xi showed some foresight. His writing efforts indicated that he knew the value of communicating in a direct and accessible way. 'Official speak' had been a persistent bane of political leaders from the time of Mao, and Mao himself had complained about it in the 1940s, writing about the need to speak lucidly and succinctly. Even so, as officials became more defined as a class of their own, they seemingly devised a whole new dialect. This language was brimming with buzzwords and was characterised by a specific way of talking. Every phrase needed to include the words 'Chinese characteristics', creating a clunky, elongated and unnatural mode of expression. Some Marxist–Leninist terminology needed to be used, as well as references to socialism. Under Jiang and Hu, cascades of data and statistics were added to this already indigestible brew. By 2007, Hu's speech at the Party Congress held that year went under the turgid title of 'Hold high the great banner of socialism with Chinese characteristics and strive for new victories in building a moderately prosperous society in all respects'. Slogans were trooped out and repeated so often that they became background noise, with no one understanding them, nor caring what they really meant. This only served to deepen the gap between officials and the people they were meant to be working on behalf of. In June 2005, Xi noted that 'many cadres don't connect with people and respect people's work. A small proportion of them couldn't seem to even talk to people.' They had, Xi observed, 'a silent attitude, and acted like they were deaf or mute'. A month later, he returned to the theme, though this time about writing. 'Officials,' he said, 'have acquired the bad habit of writing long essays, and then giving long speeches, with no content.' Speaking succinctly, deeply, attractively and with rich and effecting content was important. Cadres who believed in the party needed to convey that faith and use their words to sell it to the people around them.

Xi's second theme in the Zhejiang years, after the need for officials and the party to be clean, was economics. This is unsurprising in view of the importance of economic success in the party's performative legitimacy, as it remained in power based on its ability to produce real, tangible outcomes. Xi largely accepted the orthodoxy of the time, which was to embrace as much foreign investment as possible because of the other rewards that it brought. 'Foreign investment,' he said on 12 August 2003, 'is not just about capital but about knowledge, ability and technology.' If his outlook on life as a leader could be broadly characterised as being centred on the people, with constant references to the need of service and of placing people at the heart of policymaking, then the same was true in business and economic development. As he stated on 15 February 2005: 'Development means not being able to carry on going along the same old road. It means placing people at the heart of everything.' Economic success should serve human development, not the accumulation of wealth for the sake of it. Cadres needed to behave in accordance with their own publicly stated principles and regulations, because trust in them was economically important. On 15 September the same year, Xi declared that trust was needed in all areas of society, from government to business. GDP was a priority. The figure of 9 to 10 per cent growth a year issued by the government was a powerful symbol of its success, at least in materially improving society. But in February 2004, Xi noted that 'while we need to keep an eye on GDP growth, not everything has to be done for GDP'.

Protecting the environment was also key, as well as constructing a good society and maintaining social stability.

Strikingly, it is clear that Xi bought into a strategic long-term vision during the time he was in Zhejiang, in ways that went beyond simply guarding local and more self-centred interests. On 18 March 2004, he wrote of how 'in the current century, the first twenty years will be a period of quick economic growth in China, and the era of the maturing of the socialist market economy'. This was a period that needed to be used well in order to bring about 'the renaissance of our great country and race'. One couldn't make mistakes over this period; one false step and the whole project would fail. 'We need,' Xi said, 'to have an historic spirit.' Did Xi have any notion of his future prospects as a central leader, and as the main leader of the country for the second decade of the timescale he was referring to? It is impossible to say. But he certainly spoke with a confident sense of historic inevitability and national destiny. His words resembled language used a few years earlier by Jiang Zemin, who led the country in the early 2000s. He had also talked about the period up to 2020 being one of strategic opportunity for the country, as the US remained distracted by issues in the Middle East and elsewhere, leaving China to concentrate on developing its own capacity. The difference now was that those opportunities were closer to hand.

Xi was also aligned with the Hu leadership in his focus on rural development, even though he referenced it far less than, for instance, the need to observe discipline in the party or care for the environment. One case in point was in April 2005, when he demanded that more be done to close the gap between the two Chinas. Rural China had developed dramatically since the 1980s, with farmers allowed to introduce agricultural innovations that freed up large numbers of farm labourers to work in other areas of the economy. But it had also created a process where cities became more and more favoured in terms of growth, facilities and governance, while parts of the countryside, even a wealthy province such as Zhejiang, remained comparatively impoverished and backward. In the latter part of the decade, the Hu leadership went on to remove a tax on farmers and treat them more favourably. In many ways, this was one of the principal achievements of this era. Despite the references to the eradication of rural poverty while Xi was in Zhejiang, his leadership from 2012 could be characterised better as one that placed the Chinese urban middle class, rather than rural dwellers, at the heart of its political programme. This was because the emerging middle class was the fastest expanding demographic, and much of the government programme seemed to be to ensure as many people as possible moved from the countryside to towns or cities in order to join them. The census of 2021 underlines this, showing that the proportion of people who lived in cities had risen to 65 per cent, compared to 50 per cent at the time of the 2010 census.[8]

Perhaps with an eye to this newly emerging demographic, Xi was interested in promoting sectors like tourism, particularly environmental tourism in Zhejiang, something he referred to more than once in October 2004. At the end of 2005, he demanded that China create its own brands as a means of giving itself pride and self-confidence. In alluding to the whole philosophical basis of the Chinese development model being promoted at this time, Xi was unapologetic, stating on 23 December 2005 that 'Western industrialised civilisation was built on the basis of a few growing rich and many being poor'. China, he went on, 'has to avoid this'. This was a brave thing to say at a time when most observers agreed that the country was experiencing unprecedented and rising levels of inequality. It was this, more than any other factor, that lay behind the social conflict across the country and drove the Hu administration to talk of a 'harmonious society' where people worked closer together. As Xi had stated on 25 December that year, society would become more unstable as it became wealthier. Maintenance of stability has been the fundamental challenge of Xi's time in power. It is one of the main reasons why the crackdown on social groups like dissidents and activists has been so harsh, and why state resources have been poured into mass surveillance of public opinion and actions to try to pre-empt any potentially threatening occurrences. At the annual party conference on economics held in December 2022, the use of the word 'stability' in the final statement doubled in use compared to the year before. Stability is an omelette worth smashing many eggs for in Xi's China. Ironically, the obsession with stability at all costs has become almost destabilising, as shown by the huge geopolitical costs incurred by the crackdown in Xinjiang.

One other core theme from Xi's Zhejiang years was the call to improve the quality of growth rather than only increasing GDP no matter how it was distributed or the environmental costs. Xi demanded that the technology sector in Zhejiang be upgraded and the country become less dependent on outside imports. He wanted local companies to improve their use of technology, in particular, and for the province's logistics to be strengthened. In March 2005, he also required that the quality of inward investment from abroad be bettered, and that local companies in return become more adept at internationalising by exporting their manufactured goods, investing and promoting their brands abroad. Xi had no issue with increasing imports. As he said on 13 March that year, imports brought in good quality technology and ideas, which contributed to the mission of the party to improve people's lives.

That same month, Xi recognised that China was no longer in the phase where its greatest asset was plentiful cheap land on which to build factories and limitless cheap labour to supply them with, churning out goods for export. Instead, it now needed to cultivate creative, inventive people and acknowledge their entrepreneurial capacity. Jiang Zemin, president until 2003, had allowed private businesspeople to become party members in 2002, as part of his Three Represents idea, which saw businesspeople as important economic assets and therefore supporters of the party mission to grow, alongside intellectuals ('advanced productive forces') and the general population of the country. These 'red capitalists', as they were labelled, were well represented in Zhejiang and were a crucial network for Xi to have onside.

After discussions around the economy, the other main theme of Xi's Zhejiang articles was environmentalism and sustainability. While mentioned nowhere near as frequently as party discipline and cadre behaviour, Xi returned to these ideas relatively frequently between 2003 and 2005. On 8 August 2003, for instance, he stated that protecting the environment was not merely an option but a necessity. Everyone in society needed to think of their long-term future. 'There is only one world,' Xi said, 'and only one environment. Climate change has no limits.' Xi showed in this and other similar statements over the Zhejiang period that he recognised that fast industrialisation, particularly since the early 1980s, had taken a devastating toll on the natural environment, a situation that was now becoming critical. Once again, this recognition of the importance of environmentalism was more than merely rhetoric. At the UN climate change conference in 2009 in Copenhagen, China was criticised for being unwilling to accept high emissions caps and demanding that the developed world take the lead. Once Xi was in power, at the 2015 climate change conference in Paris, the country's attitude became much more supportive. While President Trump was a climate change sceptic, and later withdrew the US from the Paris Agreement, Xi was able to craft a much more positive, proactive position for China on this vital issue. Even after the geopolitical challenges of the Covid-19 pandemic, and the impact this has had on Sino-American relations since 2020, China has been largely on the same page as the other major international players in terms of combatting climate change derived from human activity. Despite this, at COP26, both China and India wanted less ambitious targets for phasing out fossil fuel use to be formally added to the final communique. China has committed to a series of goals to bring down emissions, the most recent of which, in September 2021, saw Xi promise the UN General Assembly to not build any coal-fired power stations abroad, a significant move in view of China's key role in constructing so many of these globally.

With extreme weather events increasing, including the floods in central China in July 2021, which led to over 300 fatalities, the question is how much more ambitious China can and should become in this area.

Xi referred to the importance of communication as one of the principal skills necessary for a successful cadre in a leadership position. That he produced these short statements so frequently during his time in Zhejiang and published them both online and in print proves that he saw the opportunity to speak to the wider, different audience offered by the internet and emerging social media. The language he used in these essays was plain and unadorned, while showing a trait that would become more pronounced in his references to classical Chinese sources and displays of wider learning. The question of audience is important to consider here. Xi's focus on party loyalty and discipline, and his attacking of corruption, was directed at fellow officials. But this was also good politics on his part, largely because these themes chimed with the wider public, who had become irritated at how officials and the party were increasingly like a privileged elite far removed from the rest of society.

The sheer repetitiveness of this part of Xi's message is arresting. He was, at this time, only one of several dozen provincial party bosses. In Beijing, there were certainly occasional references to the need for cadres to behave, but nothing in Hu

Jintao or Wen Jiabao's public pronouncements came close to being as consistent and persistent on this theme as Xi was. We don't often speak of personal conviction mattering much in Chinese politics, where the assumption is that a collectivist ethos prevails. And yet, on this particular issue, all the evidence is that Xi's words sprang from something approaching a conviction, that existed before and after he came to national power. Over a decade later, in a speech on 5 January 2018, Xi stated that elite leaders 'at provincial and ministerial level must be true believers of the ideals of Communism and socialism with Chinese characteristics'.[9] This notion of 'true believers' is a telling one. For a Communist Party presiding over a country with more dollar billionaires than anywhere except the US, where inequality is rampant and capitalism seems to have prevailed in its most predatory, ruthless manner, the notion that party officials had any faith at all was an increasingly novel one. And yet, Xi's constant references to the need to believe in the party and its mission, to speak and act consistently and to internalise this belief system imply that he did stand by these beliefs back then, and that he was confident enough to speak so loudly about them, despite his relatively junior status at the time.

That Xi staked all his political capital and commitment on the party is clear. On 9 March 2005, he said simply that 'the party is the most faithful representative of the broad masses of the people. It is the blood that flows through the body.' But why should the party matter to broader society? On that, too, Xi was firm: 'People don't care about GDP on its own. They care about what they eat and wear, their business, the education of their children, what will happen when they fall ill, and how to look after the old.' Here we can see Xi speaking as politicians do everywhere. The party matters because of service to the people; its main function is evaluating people's needs and then devising ways of fulfilling these.

There is nothing radical about this sort of mindset. It is appropriate for a worthy, obedient administrator. Why would this sort of approach make Xi stand out enough to be elevated, as he was in 2007 at the Party Congress that year, to a position in the Politburo Standing Committee? Perhaps the best answer to this is to note that the most impressive thing from Xi's Zhejiang days is not what he said – the content is largely conservative, cautious and very orthodox – but how he said it. There are persistent references to the need to preserve social stability, proving that the Communist Party was no longer revolutionary in its outlook. Xi is punctilious in referring to the Hu leadership and its ideology of 'scientific development'. His language and discourse are also very conventional, albeit unusually direct. The most unusual aspect of Xi's words from the Zhejiang years is their confidence and ambitious tone. Thus the lacerating attacks on official corruption are unambiguous and stark, as they would be when Xi became president over half a decade later, rather than being clothed in standard officialese with its ambiguities and abstract nature. The party, he stated on 27 December 2004, was not only in the business of improving the material conditions of people. It was also responsible for bettering their spiritual condition. Cadres need to be advocates of hope and optimism, showing that challenges could be converted into opportunities and that tough situations could be overcome. From prevailing over inequality to addressing environmental issues, to creating international Chinese brands and to improving the educational and social level of people, Xi's tone is consistently aspirational. So too is his absolute commitment to the idea of a national mission of rejuvenation, and of a China that could face the world on equal terms, moving beyond mere survival towards prosperity.

For all his confident, assertive tone, Xi was merely a competent local leader. He had plenty of experience, in various areas from party to government functions, but there was nothing earth-shattering about his actions in these roles. Nor, for that matter, did the outside world accord him a huge amount of interest. Only after he appeared in the leadership line-up for the Politburo in October 2007 was much attention paid to him. Two years later, in a cable subsequently published by WikiLeaks, a member of the American embassy in Beijing was told by a US-based childhood friend of Xi that he was 'exceptionally ambitious', confident and focussed, and that he had his 'eye on the prize' from early adulthood.[10] In this narrative, 'going to the provinces was his only path to central power'. Even so, these accounts all appeared after his appearance as a potential power player. What is striking is that there was almost no commentary like this even towards the end of Xi's time in Zhejiang from international media or analysts focussing on China. The wider world was bewildered that someone so ordinary on the surface could enjoy such a meteoric rise. Evidently, Western commentators had missed something and would have to do their homework on who this figure was and what he represented. As the next chapter shows, they were in for a very sharp surprise, because from the moment Xi was rewarded with the top job, his words, his actions and his bearing showed he meant business – and he meant to do that business very quickly.

CHAPTER FOUR

Xi in the Centre: His Time in Power – 2007–2017

O n 15 November 2012, several weeks after its expected date of mid-October, the Eighteenth Party Congress of the Communist Party of China was coming to its culmination. I remember gazing at a television screen in a hotel lobby in Beijing; a few streets away, in the Great Hall of the People beside Tiananmen Square, journalists were waiting nervously. After a long delay, the moment was approaching when the leadership team would walk out before the world's cameras and finally, after months of fevered speculation, it would be confirmed who was in the Standing Committee of the Politburo. However, the time of the expected announcement came and went. I wondered what was causing the hold-up, studying my Twitter feed to see if any announcement had been made, and then looking back at the television screen, which still showed an empty stage. I imagined a fraught meeting in some back room, maybe even people shouting at each other, jockeying for their final positions before trooping out before the world. Close to noon, an hour later than scheduled, the door beside the stage opened. Seven men moved expressionlessly through to take their places before the cameras. Xi stood at their head. Whatever last minute problems existed, they had obviously been ironed out. He was now certainly the leader of the Communist Party, the position from which everything else in China flowed. He had won the top spot. We were now living in the Xi era.

A great deal was at stake for whoever finally got the top job. The winner would be in charge of a country that had quadrupled its wealth in the decade since 2002 and was now the second largest economy in the world, having overtaken Japan two years before. With a fifth of the globe's population, and over 10 per cent of its global GDP, everything had changed for China since the previous transition of power except for one thing – the structure of the Communist Party, where real control was concentrated in the hands of a tiny number of people. The winner of the fight to be pre-eminent in November 2012 would take all. In this event, there were to be no runner-up prizes.

It is important to dwell briefly on the lead-up to this moment. Xi's emergence as a front runner in the party at the Seventeenth Party Congress in 2007 had been something of a surprise. But in the months before the 2012 congress, once secure in his central leadership position, Xi was a prime candidate in the hierarchy to succeed Hu.* Much of the uncertainty of five years before had evaporated. His ascension was received wisdom, though it would not have been found written down anywhere in the party's constitution. The only general guiding idea, though it was unwritten, was that in order to institutionalise the party processes and ensure it didn't fall prey to the whim of one man, as it had under Mao, all senior leaders had to observe two five-year time limits for top positions, retiring at the first congress to be held after they passed the age of 68. In 2012, having met both of these criteria, the question was therefore not whether Hu Jintao would go, but how.

In retrospect, there were clues of Xi's status as a possible replacement for Hu a few years earlier – even though, at the time of the events, these were interpreted cautiously. Xi was still seen as just one of a group of potential contenders, rather than the stand-alone candidate who was being groomed for succession. One major moment was when Chen Liangyu, the party boss of Shanghai city, was removed from office in early 2007 after claims of corruption and Xi was brought in from neighbouring Zhejiang to run the city for a few months. Shanghai is a hugely important place, economically but also

---

* Since 1982, congresses have been held regularly, unlike in the Mao era when they were far less frequent.

politically. It has often been seen as a stepping stone to greater things. It was here, for instance, that president and party boss from 1989 to 2002, Jiang Zemin, had worked in the decade before his surprise elevation after the student protests in 1989. Even so, precisely what Xi had done prior to 2007 to deserve him being given this high-profile new post was a mystery. In the Zhejiang years, he had passed the test of maintaining focus and discipline while running that huge province. But so had plenty of other similar officials in other areas of China that were equally important. His performance in terms of delivering economic gains and ensuring social stability was good but not remarkable. Once more we have to look to less tangible aspects of his performance – for example, his insistence since his time in Fujian in the mid-1990s that his relatives should not undertake any business dealings in the places where he was in office. Family financial dealings had compromised many other leaders but, despite being surrounded by temptation and opportunity, this had not proved an issue for Xi. He had told his brothers and sisters to keep away. This marked him out as a 'true believer' in the party mission, and was unusual behaviour in the era of China's vast growth boom.

Such habits continued in his time in Zhejiang and during his seven months in Shanghai. It was almost as though he were St Anthony in the desert, being tempted by mirages of wealth and beauty but proving his mettle by rejecting them.

Fujian offered plenty of material opportunities for those easily swayed. Zhejiang offered even more. But Shanghai was the greatest honey pot of all. As Xi's immediate predecessor, Chen Liangyu, had proved in 2007, it could fell even the toughest and seemingly most corruption-proof figures. Xi's strategy to deal with this final test was very simple: he bided his time. One person I spoke to in China at the time, who was based in Shanghai around that point, told me of their amusement when they observed how keen Xi was to keep a low profile and avoid anything that posed the slightest air of risk. His days were largely passed undertaking low-impact activities, ensuring that there would be no unfortunate hiccups before he could be sent to Beijing. It was for this reason that I had my single chance to meet him as part of a sister city delegation from Liverpool, in which I was a member, which was twinned with Shanghai. Needless to say, our discussion of cultural, football and heritage links posed no potential danger. We were, in that sense, the perfect delegation for him, focussing on the Beatles and Everton rather than geopolitics and questions about human rights and political reform.

Xi's reward came quickly. At the Seventeenth Party Congress in October 2007, after only seven months in Shanghai, the curtains leading to the main stage of the Great Hall of the People parted to show him emerge as number five in the nine-strong hierarchy – the same curtains he would walk through as top dog five years later. More important than his rank was the detail that the five figures that preceded him would all be over retirement age by the next congress. And, crucially, he was one place ahead of his main rival by then, Li Keqiang, which meant he was higher in the pecking order. The opacity of party processes where elite leadership choices are concerned meant that no one could be sure of Xi's eventual success at the time. Of the party's many secrets, those about leadership selection are among the best guarded. But this was the first and strongest evidence that the man who had failed to make full membership of the Central Committee a decade before had achieved a transformation in his fortunes. The Xi era began in 2012. However, the road to it started in October 2007.

From 2007 to 2012, Xi was finally based in Beijing, after decades away from the city. He was made vice-president, a principally diplomatic post that exposed him to overseas travel and foreign leaders. He became head of the Central Party School, the think tank and education centre based in the capital, which has a huge influence on party ideology and propaganda. He was also placed in charge of the Olympics, which were held in August 2008. In each case, he did an adequate job. Much of the preparatory work for the latter had already been done by the time he arrived, in the years following 2001 when China was awarded the games. The vast budget, in excess of $40 billion, used to rebuild large parts of the capital to host this event had already been spent. Xi's job was to get everything over the finishing line. But beyond this, he was largely kept away from the more complex issues of the late Hu era: the fight against the impact of the global economic crisis of 2008 was left to economists under the premier in charge of the government and economy, Wen Jiabao; the management of the escalating protests in Tibet and Xinjiang lay at Hu Jintao's own door, as the only person who had direct executive control over both the party and the military; and finally, the daily fight to keep the lid on a country that seemed to become more fractious as it grew richer belonged to Zhou Yongkang's fiefdom as head of security. As Mao Yushi, a widely admired economist wrote in a Chinese language book at this time, the country was a wealthier one, but a more and more worried one. 'Where has the anxiety of Chinese come from today?' he asked, citing a raft of issues from economic pressures, expensive housing, lack of job security and rising environmental pollution.[1] Against these huge changes, the government seemed to deploy a single approach – to continue to grow the economy so that, finally, there would be enough money to placate everyone. 'All the Communist Party has in the end is money,' a friend in China remarked to me around 2007. 'Forget everything else.' At that time, money seemed enough.

Over these five years, Xi maintained a sphinx-like inscrutability. But one event, around 2009, revealed that under this indecipherable exterior lay something punchier and less passive. On a visit to Mexico that year, he was caught on camera complaining about foreigners 'with full bellies' always criticising his country and picking faults with it. He was evidently not someone with a slavish, awed attitude towards the wider world. In view of this, it is not surprising that, once in office, Xi's demand was that his country's officials and leaders take a proactive and confident stand in dealing with the outside world. The Xi era marks the end of the period of China having a feeling of inadequacy and a lack of confidence about their own culture and national standing before other states. This, for his critics, is one of his greatest crimes. But internally, it is a position that makes absolute political sense.

This assertive, combative attitude towards the rest of the world was shaped by the 2008 Olympics. If there were ever a case of total cognitive dissonance in geopolitics, this was it. It was as though there were two separate games – the one that the Chinese saw, and the one witnessed by the rest of the world. Despite the expense and commitment China had shown in hosting the event, the global press was critical before a single medal had been awarded, highlighting the Tibet protests that took place in April that year and labelling the event the 'genocide' games.[2] While this was going on, party propagandists in China complained that their country was not being given a fair hearing. Their policies, they explained, had led to many of the world's poor being lifted out of poverty. The international media reporting remained limited and polarised – coming back to those two standard storylines explained in Chapter One, either viewing the country as a lucrative source of business opportunities, or as a place of injustice, human rights abuses and brutality. Into this narrative was plumped an event as huge in meaning for China and the rest of the world as the Olympics, which tested the adequacy of these simplistic views to their limits. For a leader like Xi, what should have been a moment for the world to celebrate the successes of China's previous three decades was marred by complaints and criticism from outsiders. No wonder, then, that by 2009 Xi regarded foreigners as people with bellies full of food and mouths full of complaints.

Despite the efforts by the Hu administration to make the transition of power a non-event, lulling the world to sleep as it happened with boring pronouncements and an attitude of business as usual, the very final months of Xi's ascent took place over a set of confusing events between 2011 and 2012, with twists and turns worthy of a Hollywood action film. Chinese elite politics seldom catches the imagination of the outside world. This is because of the generic nature of Chinese politicians, at least in terms of outwards appearances (who are almost always the same age, same gender, from the same ethnic background and even dress in same style of suits and ties). But during this period, stories started to appear of power struggles, attempted coups and even that Xi had been injured in an assassination attempt.[3] At the centre was the palpable ambition of a fellow member of the historic elite, Bo Xilai. Bo's father, Yibo, had been an even more prominent figure under Mao and Deng than Xi's own father. Bo junior was, in many ways, the great alternative to Xi. He was urbane and handsome, with a decent command of English. He was also a tremendous self-publicist, more than Xi's equal in terms of confidence and self-belief. Earlier in his career he had been a leader in the north-east of the country, attracting plaudits for his ability to woo foreign business investment in Dalian city, where he was mayor, and in Liaoning province, where he had served as governor. As minister for trade during a crucial phase in the relationship between the European Union and China in the mid-2000s, when the two were struggling over market access, he had managed to smooth over some tricky disputes regarding textiles and tariffs. Finally, as a provincial leader from 2007 in Chongqing, a vast urban area in the south-west of the country, he had undertaken a series of bold campaigns, clamping down on mafia and illegality in the city and inspiring the public with nostalgic 'red song' singalong events, reminiscent of the Mao years. All of this grabbed domestic and international headlines. For many who met him, Bo was the real deal. He also gained public support by implementing very popular affordable housing policies, examining how to address inequality and by speaking the language of sustainability every bit as fluently as Xi. Perhaps most striking of all, he fulfilled the Xi criterion for an official: he didn't merely speak empty words but tried to enact real change.

It is deeply ironic that much of what Bo did from 2007 until his fall in 2012 has obvious parallels in style and content with what Xi would later do at the national level. The clampdown on mafia and anti-social elements was criticised in the international media at the time, because of the brutal treatment doled out to both suspects and their lawyers. But in terms of cleaning up the city and ensuring people followed regulations – precisely the things Xi had supported in Zhejiang – Bo was a success. So, too, was the way in which he was able to speak directly to the people, something that Xi had insisted was a core responsibility of leading cadres. As a European politician who knew Bo quite well pointed out to me in 2011, around the time the Chinese official was attracting international attention: 'Bo is the only leader in China today who appeals to people's emotions.' This was a powerful insight. It also pointed to the characteristic that most unsettled his colleagues: Bo seemed to be genuinely popular.

For the people sitting beside him in the Politburo, the body that sits at the top of the Communist Party, however, the intensity and strength of Bo's ambition was unsettling. The premier up to 2013 and, in reality, the second most powerful person in the country, Wen Jiabao, reportedly harboured a deep detestation of his junior colleague, pointedly never visiting Chongqing while Bo was in power. Xi had no such reservations. On a visit to the city as vice-president in December 2010, Xi relayed the attractiveness of what he witnessed there. Referring to the 'red songs' campaign, he stated that 'these activities have gone deeply into the hearts of the people and are worthy of praise', and that they 'were a good vehicle for educating the broad masses of party members and cadres about [politically correct] precepts and beliefs'.[4]

Ultimately, Bo was felled not by his ambition, but as a consequence of his wife, Gu Kailai, being involved in the murder of Neil Heywood, a British businessman, in late 2011. The lid was lifted when the head of Chongqing police and, in effect, Bo's chief security official Wang Lijun, dramatically fled to the US consulate in neighbouring Chengdu in February 2012, apparently carrying proof that Gu had been present when Heywood was killed in a hotel in the city.[5] His murder was reportedly due to a business deal between the two that had gone wrong.[6] The gravity of Gu's crimes ended up tarnishing Bo by association, even though there is no evidence he played a direct part in them. He managed to survive a few more weeks, before being removed from office for corruption. He was expelled from the party and imprisoned in 2013. By that time, his dream of competing with Xi for national leadership was long dead. Gu herself was convicted of Heywood's murder and given a suspended death sentence in 2012.

It is hard to imagine what might have happened had the Heywood case never occurred. For Xi, these sordid events involving murder, embezzlement and violence had brought about precisely the sort of opportunity that could now be used to his advantage. While Bo disappeared from the equation, Xi managed to accord him the compliment of using a few of his policies and populist measures, doing so in the comforting knowledge that their creator was silenced and behind bars, unable to complain.

Parallels between Mao and Xi have often been made. In some ways, the final weeks before Xi was appointed party head in 2012 had a Maoist air about them. They were reminiscent of the time towards the end of the Chairman's life in the 1970s, when unexpected events took place almost every week. Bo's fall was the most dramatic but not the only scandalous event in this period. Newspapers reported that Xi's colleague from the Standing Committee of the Politburo, Zhou Yongkang, had been involved in moves to disrupt Xi's succession.[7] Soon afterwards, in the spring of 2012, the son of a high-level aide to Hu Jintao, Ling Jihua, was killed in a car accident. The young man, Ling Gu, had been racing a hugely expensive Ferrari around one of the ring roads of Beijing, with a couple of young, reportedly naked, women in the car (who, fortunately, survived the crash).[8] In October, the *New York Times* and others reported links between Premier Wen Jiabao's wife and huge profits that had been made from diamond trading.[9] In September, during a visit by the then US Secretary of State Hillary Clinton, Xi himself disappeared for a fortnight, stirring rumours about his health. This is when the dark murmurs of assassination attempts grew loudest. It is unclear to this day exactly what took place to incapacitate him around that time.

But as I witnessed in that hotel lobby during the Party Congress in mid-November 2012, despite the turmoil and rumours of arguments and horse trading in the background, in the end, predictability was restored. In an atmosphere of almost complete calm, face impassive and unruffled, Xi walked out with his six colleagues obediently trooping behind him. This was the new Politburo. At the preceding congress, the departing president and party leader Hu Jintao had recognised China's vast material improvement over the previous five years, speaking of these phenomenal events with a wooden blandness that belied how remarkable they were. The country's economic explosion over the past decade was the greatest single act of mass enrichment the world had ever witnessed. But in keeping with his persona as someone ever vigilant against complacency and self-regard, Xi's terse first words as supreme leader showed that a new energy was in the air. He made references to China's harsh recent history, its sense of destiny and its mission to be a

great, powerful modern country. There was also a direct reference to the people, and to their centrality in party work. 'Our
people love life and expect better education, more stable jobs,
better income, more reliable social security, medical care of
a higher standard, more comfortable living conditions, and a
more beautiful environment,' he declared.[10]

But it was the party that occupied most of his attention, as
it had done ever since his time in Zhejiang: 'Our party [now]
faces many severe challenges, and there are many pressing
problems within the party that need to be resolved, especially
problems such as corruption and bribe-taking by some party
members and cadres, being out of touch with the people, placing undue emphasis on formality and bureaucracy, [which]
must be addressed with great effort.' In hindsight, this served
as a warning of what was to come. For officials, their years of
excess and personal gain were over.

If Xi's path to power were based on any manifesto or political programme, this would be it. That day he articulated one
objective – to make the party more effective as a political force
– which has framed all his subsequent actions. The party's centrality to all that Xi does is the link between his life before and
after becoming national leader. In November 2012, he stood
on a single manifesto promise: making China great again by
making the party great. The years of officials feasting out in
luxury restaurants or going on multiple visits abroad every year

to inspect the shopping malls of Paris, London and New York at public expense, of siphoning off multiple millions of dollars of money to their overseas bank accounts and acting with complete impunity against the very laws they were meant to uphold, were about to come to an abrupt end.

It quickly became evident that Xi was firmly in control. In his early period in power, he used a different tone of language to his predecessor – sharper, more concrete, more personal. He conveyed a new narrative for the country as it moved towards great power status, derived from the years of wealth creation of the previous decade. The 'China Dream' concept and its associated publicity campaign, which was introduced in 2012, was among the most prominent, presenting the idea of improved living standards being within reach of everyone, not only the elite, and which the party was meant to be delivering to the people, rather than creating for itself. Xi was obviously keen to speak directly to the Chinese in ways that Hu had shown little interest in. He had talked before of the need to attend to the grass roots of society. In his statement at the Party Congress on 15 November 2012, he referred to officials 'being out of touch with the people'. In the first months of his leadership, therefore, he addressed this by undertaking publicity tours during which, among other things, he visited a dumpling restaurant in Beijing. The official newspaper, *China Daily*, described the event: 'Chinese President Xi Jinping showed off the common touch on Saturday with a surprise visit to a steamed bun restaurant in Beijing, where he paid for his food and chatted happily to surprised customers.' It went on: 'In pictures widely shared on China's Twitter-like microblogging service Sina Weibo, and confirmed by state media, Xi could be seen lining up for his food and posing for photographs, apparently not surrounded by the high security which normally accompanies visits by top leaders.'[11] *Xi Dada* was truly a man of the people, it seemed. In addition to the photos of Xi eating at a modest eatery, surrounded by ordinary customers, there were also clampdowns on officials blowing large sums of money on luxury restaurants and meals – these were so effective that five-star hotels in cities across China experienced a major slowdown in their revenue.[12] Some were bankrupted and had to close. The imperative was to eat 'four dishes and one soup', in official parlance, rather than, as had become the norm for some officials, sitting at a table groaning with delicacies, most of which went to waste.[13]

Xi's lifestyle itself was also used to promote this message of simplicity. One article, originally reported by the Chinese state media but now deleted, stated: 'Chinese President Xi Jinping eats breakfast before dawn. He speaks in a "bold, down-to-earth manner" … And the head of state is incredibly diligent: While others are gathering for family dinners or watching TV, Xi is still burning the midnight oil.'[14] A picture issued in 2014 showed him standing in a field, wearing rolled-up trousers and holding his own umbrella, looking like a normal resident of the countryside. This awareness of the importance of images and words and their political use in Chinese propaganda is hardly new. But the insistence on Xi, the son of a member of the political elite, being seen as down to earth and diligently working for the good of the people was almost relentlessly consistent. It came across in the words he used when meeting a foreign business delegation later in the decade, when he said that 'running such a huge country is a grave responsibility and it brings arduous work. I will fully commit to the people and never fail them. I am ready to put aside my own interest and devote my all to China's development.'[15] This sublimation of Xi to the great task he was now involved in – bringing about the culmination of the modern rejuvenation of the country – had an almost cinematic quality. It was as though the population and the rest of the world were an audience watching a carefully crafted piece of drama, where nothing could go wrong nor any part of the narrative deviate from the script. The question was who precisely was directing this grand new blockbuster, and whether it was Xi, or a whole committee of screenwriters, who were writing the material being performed.

While these campaigns were striking in intensity, none of the specific actions Xi took nor the stories he told were novel. In fact, they were deliberately well-established, and developed from long-standing previous iterations of the China story crafted by the Communist Party since 1949. The stress was on continuity, and legitimisation through this continuity, rather than the disruptiveness of new ideas and policies. Reinforcing these lines of continuity, Xi followed in his predecessor's footsteps, visiting the famous special economic zone of Shenzhen in December 2012 and remarking on the enormous significance of this place in the country's history of development, as Hu had. In 1980, Shenzhen had been a relatively quiet fishing community, but its proximity to Hong Kong meant it could be exploited. During the period 1979 to 2017 it had experienced an average annual growth rate of 22.4 per cent.[16] The district's population surged from 30,000 to over 10 million between 1979 and 2019. Shenzhen was seen as almost sacred terrain, proving that China could succeed at capitalist levels of modernisation and advancement, while still maintaining a one-party socialist system. But in order to show continuing links with the countryside, in the same month that he travelled to Shenzhen, Xi visited the impoverished Baoding area in the central northern Hebei province. Hu Jintao had engaged in a similar exercise a few years before when, in November 2008, he had stayed the night in a remote village in Shaanxi. The media had reported that 'Hu spent the festival night with villagers, having meals and joining in festive activities including a traditional dance'.[17] Those who remember Xi's inexpressive predecessor, with his almost pathological lack of emotion, may find this image quite hard to visualise.

As well as continuity with Hu's time in power, early on the Xi leadership put a strong emphasis on the idea of the party and the country being on a joint mission to achieve a successful and historic national renewal. The message was unambiguous: no unified party, no chance of national rejuvenation. A world without the unifying function of the party would be a return to the bitterly divided, chaotic and impoverished past China had experienced in the years before 1949, at the hands of the Japanese and other colonisers. The most important statement conveying this message came when Xi attended an exhibition on the theme of 'The Road to Rejuvenation', at the National Museum in central Beijing on 29 November 2012. Here he referred to the standard story of China's modern history, one where 'the Chinese people went through hardships as gruelling as "storming an iron-wall pass". Its sufferings and sacrifices in modern times were rarely seen in the history of the world. However, we Chinese never yielded.' Now 'we have finally embarked on the right path to achieve the rejuvenation of the Chinese people', Xi declared.[18] It was on this occasion that one of the core slogans of the Xi era, the 'China Dream', had its first outing.

A few weeks later, in another nod to the accepted historic narrative that he saw himself as a part of, Xi celebrated the

120th anniversary of the birth of Mao Zedong. At a symposium on 26 December, he discussed the concepts behind Mao's thought, such as Chinese destiny being decided by Chinese people and the need to have the party at the centre of national life. These ideas were of enduring value, Xi believed. They consisted of 'seeking truth from facts, the mass line and independence'.[19] Mao the dictator, the man responsible for imprisoning Xi's father, and the trauma that possibly caused the suicide of his half-sister, the man whose decisions meant that Xi himself had been forced to leave Beijing as an adolescent and live in the countryside for seven years in miserable circumstances, appears under a wholly different guise in these statements. Here, Mao is seen instead as the great founder, central to the legitimacy of the party, even in an age so utterly different to the one in which he ruled over China. The country was still in the early stages of socialism, as it had been in Mao's time. Officials therefore needed to 'promote theoretical innovation based on practice' as Mao taught them. They particularly needed to remember the notion of what Mao called the 'mass line', where the party represented all people in society and had to build a vast joint consensus. People here 'are the creators of history' before whom leaders 'are always students'; that their collective voice, which only the party fully understands, is the sole one that should be listened to. Finally, Mao had taught the iron rule that still needed to be adhered to: 'Chinese affairs must be dealt with and decided by Chinese people themselves.'

A lengthy biography of Xi was issued by the state media a few weeks after he came to power. This hadn't happened for either Hu a decade earlier or for Jiang Zemin, when he was appointed in the chaos after the 1989 uprising. In Xi's Xinhua-issued tale, his 'tough childhood' in the countryside was deployed to embed the notion that here was no remote leader, but someone whom Chinese people could see as one of their own. 'Xi,' the profile breathlessly stated, 'has expressed his deep feelings for the people on many occasions, saying for example, "How important the people are in the minds of an official will determine how important officials are in the minds of the people." His love of the people stems from his unique upbringing.'[20] This 'unique upbringing' formed a major part of the 'selling' of this new leader's persona and its connection to the existing party narratives. The underlying message was unmistakable: here was someone who had earned his right to be in this position. Despite appearances, Xi was not some entitled member of the elite. He had suffered and seen real life. He had, to use that crucial word, authenticity.

An alternative view was provided in the sceptical note, published by WikiLeaks, detailing the account of Xi's childhood friend who spoke to the American embassy official in the late 2000s. In their view:

Xi is a true 'elitist' at heart ... believing that rule by a dedicated and committed Communist Party leadership is the key to enduring social stability and national strength. The most permanent influences shaping Xi's worldview were his 'Princeling' pedigree and formative years growing up with families of first-generation CCP [Chinese Communist Party] revolutionaries in Beijing's exclusive residential compounds. Our contact is convinced that Xi has a genuine sense of 'entitlement', believing that members of his generation are the 'legitimate heirs' to the revolutionary achievements of their parents and therefore 'deserve to rule China'.[21]

However, a story is just a story. Xi's enablers, those in the elite who were now committed to his political fortune, needed to perform the true alchemy of propagandists. They had to tell the stories in a compelling manner, appealing to deep emotions in the targeted audience, in ways that the hearers themselves might not even be conscious of. *Xi Jinping Tells Stories*, the 2017 book produced by the official party news agency, divided these first talks of the Xi era into those for the outside world and those aimed at a domestic audience. 'Whoever tells the best stories, wins the masses, and then has the power of being listened to, the power of speech,' the introduction stated.

Xi could appeal to his audience by making sure there was a direct link between his life story and the party's own extraordinary and dramatic rise to power. Like his *New Sayings from Zhejiang*, these were short, direct pieces of a similar style to those in Mao's 'Little Red Book', *Quotations from Chairman Mao*, which was published in 1964, and widely read during the Cultural Revolution a few years later. *Xi Jinping Tells Stories* also uses well-known fables, such as that on which the Beijing opera *Farewell My Concubine* is based (rather than the 1985 novel by Lilian Lee and the 1993 film adaptation by Chen Kaige). This story recalls the battles waged over 2,000 years ago to unify and strengthen imperial China, establishing the Han dynasty, one of the most successful and longest lasting in all Chinese history. In Xi's retelling, the power of faith in the party is extolled in order to maintain the country's strength and integrity, as is the need to be clear-sighted about adversaries. This group, the corrupt and malfeasant, would become major targets of Xi's administration – portrayed as the enemy within, who were undermining the whole project of national renewal. Like most storytellers, Xi and the party well understand that depicting a world with definite boundaries between good and evil, and having vividly drawn enemies, is always an effective means of grabbing people's attention.

This was the reasoning behind Xi's 'anti-corruption campaign', as it was called in Western media, being framed in terms of a struggle between good and evil. It was as though the country were some chaotic town that had been run to ruin, and Xi were the sheriff who had arrived to clean it up. Anti-corruption campaigns were nothing new. From the 1980s onwards, there had been sporadic attempts to tackle corruption in China, but the breadth and tone of the one under Xi was different. A man called Wang Qishan was put in charge of the whole process; he was a formidable and widely respected operator, someone who had put out major fires in the past, such as dealing with the ruptures over misconduct and embezzlement in the build-up to the 2008 Olympics when he was mayor of Beijing. An historian by training, who had also worked at the Chinese Academy of Social Sciences before becoming an official, Wang was the chief interlocutor between the Obama White House and the Hu leadership. Observing him during a meeting looking at party work and the corruption campaign I took part in with foreign and Chinese scholars in 2014, I could see why he was regarded with such fear. He chose his every word carefully, and his immense self-control created an aura of power and authority around him. At that meeting, Wang spoke in a quiet, soothing voice – so that one almost had to lean towards him to hear his words. Every phrase he used seemed laden with hidden meaning and import. Like many charismatic politicians, he showed the ability to control the pace of events and keep his listeners attentive to what he said. The clampdown on corruption was not a campaign, he said, but a life and death struggle. It would never end. It would stretch from party officials to all other parts of society, because in the end everyone had duties to the party. Pausing and looking around the room, he asked why the party was doing this. Because, he explained, answering his own question, the greatest issue the country faced was inequity and inequality. That is what most angered and upset people. Seeing tangible injustice and unfairness with their own eyes, where some members of society could act with complete impunity because they were party members, and others could accumulate illicit wealth, while the majority struggled and barely survived. As Wang spoke, I imagined what it would be like to have him appear in your life if you were an official under investigation. With those soothing tones, that quiet, commanding voice accusing you of being a traitor and reprobate, I could envisage all too well how terrifying that experience could be. That day, I left the meeting deeply relieved I was only an unimportant visiting researcher, and not someone who would ever be remotely significant enough to attract Mr Wang's very unwelcome attention.

Wang had reason to speak with such self-belief. By the time I was part of the delegation that met him, the campaign he had spearheaded had been a public success. A few months later, I was speaking to a Chinese businessperson when the conversation turned to how the removal of so many cadres at all levels had been perceived by the public; my companion said that, from their point of view, whether one agreed with laws and regulations or not, at least now officials would have to carry them out rather than blithely ignore them, which had been the case in the recent past. China, once so anarchic and chaotic, was now a relatively predictable place to do business. That view was echoed by a lawyer in the relatively undeveloped and more remote Inner Mongolian region I spoke to at around the same time, who had despaired about local court rulings not being implemented as the region was saturated by vested interest and cronyism. Now, to their amazement, once the courts opined, decisive actions had to happen.

Wang's boss, Xi the storyteller, also framed the fight against corruption as an existential struggle. He spoke of the battle against 'tigers' and 'flies'; of the powerful leaders, small officials and those who had fled abroad feeling they would be safe there.[22] The trial of Bo Xilai and Zhou Yongkang, a member of the Standing Committee in charge of security from 2007 to 2012, and someone accused of backing Bo's claims to power, showed that the biggest of the tigers were not immune; both were sent to prison for many years. It was unprecedented that a figure as high ranking as Zhou should have this treatment meted out to them. Ling Jihua, Hu Jintao's key aide whose son had died in the car crash in 2012, was also removed. A few years later, in 2017, Sun Zhengcai, another Politburo member who had frequently been slated for promotion while head of the same ill-fated Chongqing area that had once been Bo's empire, was also dramatically felled. Wang Qishan's enforcers sent their tentacles deep across the system. General Guo Boxiong, a senior army leader and member of the Politburo and vice-chairman of the Central Military Commission (the body chaired by Xi regulating the armed forces), was arrested in 2015, expelled from the party and sentenced to life imprisonment. Ma Jian, former head of counter-intelligence in the Ministry of State Security, a department shrouded in mystery and previously regarded as almost untouchable, was also removed and imprisoned in 2016. Even those who had worked for international organisations, like Meng Hongwei, who served as the head of Interpol from 2016 to 2018, were caught up in the corruption crackdown. He was detained in 2020 while back in China and sentenced to thirteen years in prison for bribery.

These are the most high-profile cases of the Xi years; many thousands of lesser-known figures were also arrested. This number, however, was a small proportion of those investigated, and a tiny proportion of actual working officials. As American scholar Andrew Wedeman has written, to be corrupt in China is still statistically a relatively risk-free activity.[23] The trick was to create a sense of apprehension and fear by showing, in a few highly representative cases, the vast costs that were incurred if one were ever caught. The real impetus for the party giving itself such a monumental public drubbing was to fulfil Xi's promise to clean it up, and for the party to become humbler, more focussed on society, and more accountable. This may be why much of the anti-corruption campaign involved a massive dose of theatre. In real terms, it is unlikely that a self-inflicted beating would ever be as harsh as one administered by someone else. But that wasn't the point: at least the party looked as though it were trying to get its own house in order. Once this was done, it could then demand high levels of discipline from other sectors of society.

By 2015, state-owned enterprises and private sector companies were also being targeted. Strategically, the anti-corruption 'struggle' as Wang Qishan called it, certainly created enough fear and uncertainty to make party officials behave. The mere threat of the body that he headed, the Central Commission for Discipline Inspection (CCDI), appearing and undertaking investigations was enough to make most fall into line. Wang's people had almost unbridled powers to turf through material, take people into custody and do what was necessary to ensure they cooperated with investigations. There were complaints of people disappearing while they were being interrogated, and of others being mishandled and abused. As Mao Zedong once said, 'A revolution is not a dinner party.' Nor, most certainly, was being investigated by the CCDI.

Accompanying the hard and nasty business of weeding out corruption went the more routine work of party building and ideological training, which had also once been more common than in recent years. From 2013, cadres were sent to the grass roots, to villages and small towns, the most basic units of governance, to get experience. Their training was made stricter and more uniform. One official I knew in Beijing told me that they were going to be sent to Tibet in 2017. 'It will be excellent for my career,' they said, a very different response to that which an earlier generation might have expressed, who would have regarded such a posting as a form of internal exile and punishment. New digital technology was brought in to promote intellectual and behavioural conformity, including a 'Xi Jinping Thought' app, which fed cadres daily wholesome quotes and tested them on their ideological knowledge. The motive behind all of this was to address the crisis of faith in the party, and make sure that officials didn't mouth platitudes but actually acted on the beliefs they professed to stand for. Respect for the 'mass line' – a Chinese way of referring to public opinion – was important, as was a culture of better serving the people and doing more to communicate with them. Xi visited state media outlets in 2015, spoke to thinkers in the cultural and intellectual realm and targeted universities. The message was obvious. The West was not some paradise. People should not be naïve about its offers to help with Chinese political reform.

What they really wanted, Xi and his colleagues believed, was to see China become as weak as Russia had after the collapse of the USSR.

This attitude had intensified since the global economic crisis in 2008. At that time, Western capitalism had proved it did not have all the answers, not even for itself, let alone China. While Western democratic systems, universalism and federal governance models had all been examined in the past, the Chinese people could now safely conclude that such structures were irrelevant for their country. The leadership expected loyalty on this point. As Xi had said before, while consensus was being formed, new ideas and new proposals were fine. But once agreement had been reached, the discussion stopped. The Xi era has shown that debate and argument is over on the issues of Western democracy and governance. Those who want to continue to challenge Xi's orthodoxy must be prepared to face the consequences. One such figure was academic Xu Zhangrun, whose criticism of Xi and accusations of hubris and arrogance were rewarded with the loss of his job and social isolation. He was even briefly arrested in 2020 on charges of using prostitutes (which were subsequently dropped). The 'era of moral depletion' was the phrase that Xu deployed about Xi's rule in 2020.[24] But Xu's voice was a lone one, which only made his courage in speaking out all the more remarkable.

The cleansing of the party through the anti-corruption struggle, the forging of loyalty through ideological training and education, and the efforts put into messaging and propaganda continued apace. In some senses, Xu and other critics were wrong. These policies were not for Xi's own personal delectation. Even in his seemingly all-powerful position, Xi had to satisfy important groups and factions from the party elite, the military and the business and other sectors – people who could, if they felt the strategy was not going well, cause him significant problems. Real trenchant dissent has largely been manageable so far precisely because it has come from human rights lawyers and individual scholars such as Xu, who have limited domestic networks. These are groups that were already viewed by the party as potential sources of opposition long before Xi appeared. Even when a letter expressing disquiet about Xi's autocratic style of rule surfaced in 2016, reportedly from 'loyal party members', bringing it a bit closer to more dangerous territory, it was anonymous and caused barely a crack across the placid surface of the party façade.[25] It is telling that among the group that most matters to Xi for his day-to-day work – the upper levels of the elite within the party – everyone appears to remain firmly wedded to this 'collective leadership', with no fissures appearing as of the time of writing in early 2022. Deng had to deal with the new leftists in the 1980s, Jiang with the subliminal but obvious reservations of former Politburo member Qiao Shi, and Hu saw his own Premier Wen Jiabao start to muse about the necessity for political reform and democracy in China towards the end of the 2000s. Xi has had no such critical figures. The silence of those around him and immediately beside him is almost eerie. What, beyond fear, could have precipitated this?

One possible reason, which became evident from 2012 to 2017, is that Xi is definite about who is at the heart of his political project, those who would be so significant for its eventual success: the emerging middle class. This group were not easily defined when Xi came to power. The Chinese economy had changed in such a way that there were now more people than ever working in the services sector; these were no Marxist proletariats. This group owned property. They worked in management or finance, rather than factories. Many ran their own companies. Then there was the issue of the per capita income figure across China– uneven across provinces, but still creeping up across the board. By 2019 China was able to classify itself as a middle-income country with a national average per capita GDP of over $10,000 a year.[26] The middle class in this society were better educated than ever before, with more and more going to the country's growing number of universities. Forty million people were enrolled in college and degree courses by 2020, with 8.7 million graduating that year.[27] China had 225 million privately owned cars by 2021, a five-fold increase since 2009; and the number of people living in urban areas increased by 15 per cent, to almost a billion people, between 2010 to 2021.[28] This all testified to a society in flux. Historically, the party had been the vanguard of the workers and the farmers; now it needed to make room for the new middle class – Communism was serving the bourgeoisie.

This group is critical for both political and economic reasons. Around 2014, Xi's premier and his effective deputy in charge of administration, Li Keqiang, talked of a 'new normal'. The dramatically large increases in GDP that China had experienced in the previous decades were slowing down. As Xi declared in 2013, the main challenge facing China was 'unbalanced, uncoordinated and unsustainable development'.[29] The Hu administration had also recognised these issues – once more, there was nothing remotely radical about what Xi was trying to do, it was only a continuation of previous undertakings. The difference was a stronger focus on the middle class, who were greater in number and more real in potential impact in 2015 than ever before. As economic growth fell to 6.7 per cent in 2016, they had also become more important.[30] China did indeed have the world's greatest economic asset: not resources nor manufacturing capacity, but the spending power of its own people. Looking at the composition of the Chinese economy in 2017, this was unmistakable. Over 41 per cent of GDP was invested in fixed capital formation, and only 54 per cent in consumption.[31] This latter figure had remained stubbornly fixed from 50 to 60 per cent since 2003, despite repeated attempts to increase it. Hu's government had launched its fiscal stimulus programme in 2008 to respond to the financial crisis and encourage people to spend more, but this had limited impact. Even in 2022, the consumption figure has still not shifted dramatically.[32] In comparison, 81 per cent of the US economy in 2020 was in personal consumption, a figure almost a third as high as China's.

The standard explanation for why the Chinese people save so much and spend so little has been that they have historically lived in an environment of great uncertainty. The social security system is uneven and imperfect. Those who fall ill must pay large costs up front, and improvements in health insurance have not changed this. There are limited means of investing. Bank accounts give miniscule rates of return on savings deposits. In the past, the Shanghai Stock Exchange or purchasing property offered far better prospects, but there was a constant fear that they might collapse. In 2014 and 2015, the Shanghai Stock Exchange did fall dramatically, meaning many of the 75 million personal account holders lost money. This particular incident saw the Xi leadership curiously flat-footed in its response, not reacting for a number of days as though unsure what to do. Trust was a word Xi had used a lot; the issue for the new middle class was trust, or rather the lack of it. Their loyalty was not a matter of only obeying orders from the party, or even threats from it – the middle class comprised far too many people for that to succeed. The main ploy was a combination of nationalist appeal, institutional reform and a more service-orientated ethos for the government. Xi calls himself the servant of the people – but it would be more accurate to say that he is the servant of the middle class.

In this context, the campaign on party corruption was good domestic politics. But Xi was also starting to look at issues such as the rule of law. This had been a tricky area for some years; the party has never liked lawyers. As a party official told me in 2010, ultimately, the party had risen to power illegally. It regarded lawyers as disruptive, opportunist and easily politicised, and it categorically rejected American or European models, where an independent judiciary was able to issue judgments to politicians, impacting on their ability to act. China needed rule *by* law, because it wanted predictability. But it emphatically did not want rule *of* law. Ruling was the party's business. The law should keep well away.

The resulting legal reforms began in 2014, with the strengthening of property laws. Responsibility for local courts was removed from the corresponding provincial government to more senior administration, taking away potential conflicts of interest and sources of collusion. Up until this point, one section of society had always suffered for the benefit of another demographic. First the farmers had suffered, enduring low wages and poor conditions so that the cities could receive investment. In the reform era, the great sacrifices had been made by migrant factory labourers, working long hours and earning very little compared to the value of the products they were making. In Xi's middle-class China, finally, the bourgeoisie would have to work harder, contribute more in terms of consumption and, perhaps one day, even pay a far higher burden of tax revenue. This group is far more rights-conscious and voluble than the farmers or migrants had been. It needs stronger reassurances that their property rights are protected, their commercial interests are secure and the party is on their side in providing good-quality universities, public services like social welfare and pensions and healthcare services.

This group also explains some of the other striking aspects of the Xi leadership. In late 2015, vast amounts of military kit were paraded through the streets of Beijing to mark the seventieth anniversary of the end of the Second World War in Asia. The outside world was deeply unsettled by the display, but to the domestic audience this visible manifestation of their country's hard power was reassuring and satisfying. China was no longer a weak marginal country. Xi's confidence and the proactive nature of his diplomacy, compared to the low-key, more humble approach of his predecessors, appealed to this nationalist strain. The imaginations and emotions of the Chinese middle class were fired by the sight of their reju-venated, powerful, wealthy and, sometimes, feared country. Surveys such as that carried out by the Ash Center at Harvard University from 2003 to 2020 found that Xi's government enjoyed high levels of public support and satisfaction; this was due to the fact that, in the words of Tony Saich, one of the authors of the report, 'in their lived experience of the past four decades, each day was better than the next'.[33]

Unlike Japanese nationalism in the region, Chinese nation-alism has a far more shadowy modern track record. Since 1979, China has never initiated a major conflict or campaign of physical aggression on any significant scale against its neigh-bours.* But the Xi leadership has been unashamed in deploying the idea of China as a great and powerful country. Part of the 'China Dream' from 2012 relates to this set of sentiments, speaking directly to Chinese people and their aspirations to be wealthy, live prosperous lives and have the same kinds of public services, housing and living environments, and the same life opportunities, as those in developed countries like the US or in Europe. This 'dream' is not, therefore, nebulous, but one in

---

* This was the unsuccessful attack on Vietnam that year. Since then, apart from some low-level clashes in the South China Sea involving fishing craft, and somewhat primitive physical brawls with Indian sol-diers on the disputed Sino-Indian border, there has been no conflict of note.

which all Chinese can participate, as stakeholders in a country on the rise, materially displaying its new power and confidence.

Despite confusion about how best to understand it, nationalism as we are witnessing today in the People's Republic has not fallen from a blue sky. Far from it. All Chinese leaders since 1949 have shared a concept of China as a vast, ancient, inspiring ideal. In a country where there are complex, often clashing belief systems from Buddhism, to Daoism, to Confucianism, to Islam and Christianity, the vision of the great nation offers a quasi-religious ideal that can transcend and bind together these disparate faiths. China can unite behind the idea that the country has a moral right to become great, powerful and respected after its difficult modern history of instability, victimisation and suffering during events like the catastrophic Sino-Japanese War from 1937, which saw up to 20 million Chinese perish, and as many as 50 million displaced in the wide-scale destruction of this era.

Nationalism aside, Xi's onslaught had brought him huge powers. One of the main aspects of this over the 2012 to 2017 period was the vicious and devastating repression against those regarded as dissenting voices. The incident in July 2015 during which around 300 lawyers were detained on the grounds that they were using legal work to disrupt social stability has already been referred to. A similar action targeting non-government organisations followed in 2017, after a new regulation restricted the involvement of foreign partners and funding. That year, China's most famous dissident, the poet, critic and Nobel Peace Prize Laureate Liu Xiaobo, tragically died of cancer during incarceration after nearly a decade in jail. What changed was that China was now pursuing its opponents beyond its own borders. Booksellers in Hong Kong were detained, accused of peddling rumours about the Xi leadership; one individual suffered an extra-territorial kidnapping in 2015. This was despite the promise that as Hong Kongese, they would live under a different legal jurisdiction until 2047. China-based foreigners like Peter Humphrey, a British national, were apprehended over accusations of corruption. Despite consistently protesting his innocence, Humphrey was jailed for two years in 2014, and forced to appear on state television.*

Like Mao, Xi is definite about who should be seen as enemies to the national mission; they are a fundamental part of the storytelling now taking place. In one of his earliest works from 1926, 'Analysis of the Classes in Chinese Society', Mao said that, for revolution to succeed, one must work out who are your friends and who are your opponents. The same principle applies for Xi's China. Among those regarded as the

---

* Two Canadians were also detained in 2019 on charges of espionage, and only released in 2021.

most dangerous, and therefore the most savagely treated, are people and groups accused of separatism. On 1 March 2014, around 30 people were murdered at Kunming train station by what was claimed to be a group of Uyghur terrorists; an attempted suicide attack in Tiananmen Square in late 2013 also rattled the central government and the wider population. The government's response to such threats has been fierce, with a particular focus on the vast Xinjiang province, in the north-west of the country. Beginning in 2017, an estimated 1 million people of Uyghur ethnicity were detained, marking a new campaign by the party against what it claimed were the 'three evils' of terrorism, separatism and political extremism. This sparked international concern and outrage, with some condemning it as 'genocide'.[34] The availability of new forms of surveillance and facial recognition technology has led to some calling Xinjiang a large prison state.[35] However, the Chinese middle class largely supported this move by the party on the grounds of security. As of 2022, the government has remained unapologetic about its actions and unmoved by criticism from the West. This had caused countries such as the US to diplomatically boycott the 2022 Winter Olympics hosted in Beijing.

It was obvious from the start that the Xi leadership prioritised politics over economics. Even when Xi's comments superficially seem to be about economics, they largely fall into the political space, usually referring to issues around equity and the need for social cohesion. The stakes are high in the search for political stability. Since the Arab Spring in 2010 and the colour revolutions in the former USSR satellite states, the leadership in Beijing has been deeply aware that the country is living in a precarious and dangerous moment. As the decade wore on, the US witnessed rising levels of unrest, while Britain and Europe split from each other. In 2021, the world's sole remaining superpower oversaw a chaotic withdrawal from Afghanistan, leaving it in the hands of the Taliban after two decades, which led to the loss of trillions of dollars and countless military and civilian casualties. There are no good models to follow for China, nor easy allies. The decision to go it alone has already been made.

By 2017, Xi had already made clear the extent of his ambitions. An annual meeting of the party in late 2013 had set out a programme of legal and economic reform, which alluded to a timeframe of decades rather than that of one or two years. A small high-level group chaired by Xi was established at the same time, calling itself the 'Committee for Comprehensively Deepening Reform'. 'Reform' became a buzzword. In this opening five years, Xi's main focus was on getting the party into shape. Like a runner about to embark on a marathon, the party was forced to train, lose some of its bad habits, and acquire focus and discipline. Xi undoubtedly thought he had done a good job. From 2017, he and his colleagues started to speak of a 'New Era' being imminent. It was evident that they believed that the next act of the great, ambitious drama they were in had already started – a performance in which they had revealed themselves to be the screenwriters, the actors and the director. Xi Jinping Season Two had begun.

CHAPTER FIVE

Xi and the New Era – 2017–2022

In mid-2017, I visited China to speak at a couple of events; the schedule was tight and on one day I had to leave Shanghai at lunchtime and make it to Beijing by late afternoon. Only a few years earlier, attempting a journey like this would have required something close to a miracle. The train journey usually took over 12 hours; even with the new network of highways, driving took about the same length of time – and that was if the driver paid no heed to speed limits. Flying used up only two and a half hours, but getting from downtown Shanghai to one of the city's two airports, then clearing security, took at least another two hours. At the other end, it was the same process in reverse – battling through the capital's traffic or taking a chance on the underground. Leaving Shanghai at 1pm meant there was precious little chance of getting to Beijing before 8pm. And that was without the air traffic delays that blighted so many flights in the country, where only a fraction of the air space is allowed for civilian flights in favour of the military, causing severe congestion.

In Xi's second term, following the Party Congress in 2017, the high-speed rail network now covers the whole country. Like so much else, including many of Xi's principal policies, building the infrastructure was begun in the late Hu era, after 2006. But since 2012, China has built 40,000 kilometres of track, allowing trains to travel at 300 kilometres an hour or more.* In theory, it is now possible to travel from one end of the country to the other in a matter of hours. In comparison, not a single train in the US can go above 250 kilometres an hour; in the UK, as of 2022, there are less than 500 kilometres of high-speed track for use, with another line extending north from London not due to become operational for another decade or more. China's achievement is astonishing: it constructed many times more high speed rail than the rest of the world combined, in only a few years.

That day I had lunch in a hotel along the historic Bund by the water in Shanghai; I finished eating at 1pm and took one of the new underground lines that have made the city's network the longest in the world. Forty minutes later I was at

---

* A fatal 2011 train crash in Wenzhou, in which 40 people were tragically killed, meant that although speeds of over 350 kilometres an hour were perfectly possible, they were barred for safety reasons.

the high-speed rail station. The train to Beijing departed at 2pm, I arrived in the capital soon after 6.30pm and was sitting down to an evening meal by 7pm. That, too, was courtesy of the world's second longest underground network at the other end. As the train rocketed north, passing rice fields, rivers, towns, roads and wooded areas, I remember being struck by how, for a Chinese citizen, this transformation of their physical world must have been cause for satisfaction and pride. After all, as recently as the 1980s, many Chinese people's greatest dream was to own a domestically produced Flying Pigeon bicycle. These days, even Ferraris and Bentleys have become common enough to not prompt too many local jaws to drop. In 2020, despite the pandemic, 2.53 million luxury cars were sold in China.[1] After decades of struggle and toil, was China finally becoming a lucky country?

Like the Chinese physical landscape, by 2017, Xi seemed to be consumed by an even greater sense of purpose. This fresh confidence played well domestically – reinforcing this conviction that China's moment had come. Speaking as he was reappointed that year, Xi declared that, thanks to 'decades of tireless struggle', the country now stood tall in the East. 'The Chinese nation,' he went on, 'has stood up, grown rich, and become strong – and it now embraces the brilliant prospects of rejuvenation … It will be an era that sees China moving closer to centre stage and making greater contributions to mankind.'[2] His words echoed those made by Mao at the dawn of the People's Republic in 1949, when he too had said that, after decades of war and struggle, the Chinese people and nation 'had stood up'. But for Xi, unlike for Mao, there was empirical evidence that this truly was the case, rather than an emotion-fuelled aspiration; it was testified to by achievements like the high-speed rail, luxury car ownership and, ironically, the fact that now China was genuinely not only respected but feared by the West. In a perverse way, this above all was proof to the fact that the country had arrived.

Some (J.F. Kennedy among them) have pointed out that the Chinese word for 'crisis' (*weiji*) places the character for 'danger' (*wei*) next to that for 'opportunity' (*ji*). In fact, as linguists will point out, this is not the case – with *ji* having a far less precise meaning than that given to it here. Even so, this captures well the idea often attributed to Chinese leaders of believing that events have the possibility to be good or bad due to human action and intervention, rather than because of any intrinsic properties they have. Speaking confidently and powerfully, from 2017, Xi seemed to reinforce the sense created by the anti-corruption purges and his increased assertiveness in foreign affairs that he was a strongman able to re-channel fate and transform danger into opportunity. It was at precisely the same time as Xi described China as standing tall that the *Economist* carried the sobering message that he was the most powerful person in the world. 'Xi Jinping has more clout than Donald Trump,' the magazine declared. 'The world should be wary.'[3] As though to ram this home, in 2017, significant repressive measures began in Hong Kong, as did the first signs of a major security move in Xinjiang.

Had things been different at the start of Xi's time in power – had economic growth fallen unexpectedly, or relations with Japan, India or the US become more confrontational – it is interesting to wonder what type of leadership style Xi would have adopted after 2017. But a relatively good stretch of success, coupled with the anti-corruption campaign having removed his most problematic opponents, meant that by October that year Xi's political capital ran high. Then came the announcement that at the 2018 National People's Congress, China's annual parliament (as opposed to the Party Congress which meets every five years), the existing time limits of presidential terms would be scrapped, meaning Xi could continue in his role for good. 'Xi Jinping Thought' was also inscribed in the state constitution. Commentators in the West wondered whether they were seeing the rise of a dictatorship. These were politically crucial moves which carried huge symbolic weight and reinforced the image of Xi as a leader in total control. In 2009, in the WikiLeaks cable, the unnamed figure who had known Xi as a young man remarked that, while he was probably uncorruptible by material gain,

Xi was potentially corruptible by power. Was this what the world was starting to witness?

When the 2017 congress line-up eventually emerged, the leadership around Xi had been completely overhauled. Only his premier, Li Keqiang, survived. All the other figures on the previous seven-strong Standing Committee retired. But while the formidable Wang Qishan lost his Politburo place, he was given a new role as vice-president, meaning he could continue working. In this single move, the willingness of Xi to innovate and change the unspoken rules of Chinese politics to fit the new situation were made starkly clear. The informal understanding that people had to retire as soon after their sixty-eighth birthday as possible, which had started in the early 1980s as part of the reforms under Deng Xiaoping, meant that extremely capable people had been sidelined in the past. Deng himself, for example, had come into his element only in his mid-seventies. Xi's leadership was revising the unwritten rulebook. As with other rules, the fact these practices had never been written down anywhere in the first place meant changing them was easy. In this case, too, there was a healthy dose of self-interest. Xi was creating a precedent that would be very useful to him five years hence when he too, over 68, should be retiring.

The new top-level line-up were survivors of the anti-corruption struggle. It was as though they were the last men (and they were all men) standing from a huge shoot-out, in which everyone else had been eliminated. They were politicians with lengthy administrative experience but zero charisma or no substantial autonomous political power bases in their own right. Wang Huning was the most striking. An academic until the 1990s, he had played a significant role in Beijing politics since the days of Jiang Zemin, crafting and devising a series of concepts such as the Three Represents, which allowed entrepreneurs to join the Communist Party in the early 2000s; the Scientific Development ideas of Hu, which introduced the notion that the quality of economic growth was more important than quantity; and now the China Dream under Xi. His world view was underwritten by a strong sense that the West was failing, and that China's principal mission was to ensure it was not corrupted by the ills of capitalism – from inequality to the loss of the party's values. In the 1980s, he had spent a brief period as a visiting scholar in the US. A book published in 1991, curtly titled *America Against America*, summarised his conclusions of his stay. America was a declining power with a sense of cultural arrogance, but no real underlying cultural confidence. Reinforcing the sense of the Chinese enjoying thousands of years of deep cultural identity and coherence was the great thread that ran through Wang's work, and which, in Xi, met a politician deeply receptive to these ideas.

Beyond this, Xi's new group of colleagues could not easily be consigned to separate networks or internal factions, as had been the case in the past. Han Zheng is a good example: formerly mayor and then party boss of Shanghai for many years, he briefly worked with Xi when the latter was in charge of the city in 2007. He had survived in an environment of dizzying wealth and dynamism, akin to that Xi experienced in Fujian and Zhejiang, without being caught up in the various complex scams and problems the city had experienced. In 2007, when Chen Liangyu was removed from power over claims of massive corruption, along with a raft of other officials, Han was left untouched. This was reminiscent of the Lai Changxing smuggling case in Fujian, where Xi was left similarly unscathed by graft that seemed to connect to everyone else serving there. Other new figures in the line-up like Li Zhanshu and Wang Yang were veterans of provincial leadership, with the latter having led firstly Chongqing and then the vast Guangdong province. The final figure was Zhao Leji, who had combined provincial leadership with heading up the party's personnel department.

There was no single unifying characteristic shared by these figures. They were not all united by having worked with Xi in his previous career, nor were they all members of the so-called Princelings faction, with parents or grandparents who had been elite leaders in the past. For a leader keen to control the narrative, ironically, it was hard to know what the story of this line-up was telling the world. The only discernible theme was that this group seemed to have deliberately been selected to fulfil claims that the top-level Chinese leaders were faceless, generic and almost like automaton. There would be no upstaging of the real star of the show – Xi himself – here.

If one reflects more deeply, however, perhaps another more subtle narrative emerges. For a storyteller like Xi, this high-profile event was too good a chance to miss. David Runciman, the British political philosopher, has argued that, in the end, Western politicians mainly specialise in failure.[4] They constantly have to scale back their promises and come to terms with the intractable, unforgiving reality that they can never fulfil their earlier pledges. This would not be a definition that any Chinese politician today would recognise, publicly, at least. They are in the business of success and live in a world where, they believe, any problem can be solved with enough time and the right principles. In their view, society is predictable, merely a vast machine, and once the inputs, outputs and formulae are applied, things will necessarily work out. In many ways, the 2017 leadership members were engineers installed to deliver one successful outcome: to make China a middle-income country within 100 years of the Communist Party being founded. They were qualified for this role because they already had a track record of delivering success in complementary fields, from the ideological to the administrative. Importantly, they had done this while not drawing attention to themselves as individuals but, ostensibly, as obedient, loyal servants of the party. In that context, they were actors in a drama where the main theme was devotion to the party mission, almost to the point of selflessness.

In any case, in 2017, the real player more than ever was the party as a corporate body. Through the use of new technology, it could see into the hearts and minds of individuals as never before. It was able to extend itself in a wholly different way to what had been possible in the past. In the Mao period, this level of penetration may have been desired, but the technology to deliver it did not exist. By 2020, once around a billion Chinese had gravitated online, their consumer habits, their personal lives and their innermost thoughts were theoretically available. Far from being, as media mogul Rupert Murdoch claimed in the 1990s, a threat to one-party systems, increased cyber capacity has ended up providing an immense harvest, an extra source of power and influence, something that China's Communist Party has seized on with almost greedy eagerness. It no longer needed neighbourhood watch committees and spies working among the people as it did in the past. It could snoop and eavesdrop and observe from the many anonymous buildings spread throughout China where the state cyber analysts worked, producing their daily spreadsheets for leaders with hot topics and buzzwords that needed to be monitored carefully. As a Chinese journalist told me in 2015, 'Our leaders spend an hour or so a day online looking at public opinion and surveys.' Who needed to go on time-consuming, gruelling investigation tours to the countryside to check the public pulse when you could do it in an hour or so from the comfort of your own office?

Xi recognised the power of technology and its importance for the party early on. During his time in Zhejiang, he saw first-hand the creation of successful internet start-ups, like Alibaba. He had also engaged in blogging and online communication himself. In the early days of the internet, the party had been behind the curve with this new virtual world. In the 1990s, outlawed groups such as Falun Gong were able to use the internet to proselytise and to organise themselves for protests; one rally in 1999 saw thousands of followers appear, as if from nowhere, and surround the central government compound at Zhongnanhai in Beijing before a brutal government offensive stopped them in their tracks. International organisations like Google and, very early on, Facebook could ignore the physical boundaries of China as a country, and come in with sinified versions of their products to try to conquer the huge emerging internal market. During the 2008 Olympics, the party grudgingly offered to allow unfettered internet access. However, this didn't last long.

Towards the end of Hu's time in power, the party had started fighting back. It was profoundly rattled by the role that Facebook and other social media platforms played in the Arab Spring. Fang Binxing, a former president of the Beijing University of Post and Telecommunications, set up the first national system of vigilance and cyber enclosure; he was subsequently nicknamed the father of the 'Great Firewall of China'. Ironically, the Great Firewall grew from a system of eavesdropping on the telecommunication surveillance that Fang had devised for Bo Xilai, Xi's nemesis, in Chongqing around 2010, which was then extended to blocking large numbers of sites and content considered unhealthy and politically unacceptable. The implementation of the Great Firewall was the reason for Google's withdrawal from China in 2010, and it explained why, as the decade wore on, certain international websites were inaccessible in the country unless virtual private networks were used.

With Xi, this process has reached its culmination. Speaking in 2015, he referred to the country enjoying 'cyber sovereignty'. The notion that there was a global common space in the virtual world was debunked. Deeply distrustful of the motives of outside governments, and suspicious of them using the internet to infiltrate the country and infect it with subversive ideas and thinking, Xi upended the tables. Much as there were universal values for the West, which did not apply to China's unique set of convictions, so there was a universal virtual space for others if they wanted it, but China was opting out and creating its own. Bit by bit, on visiting China, I noticed that once-accessible websites were blocked unless you were using a virtual private network. After Facebook, Gmail was slowed down, then closed. The BBC was an early victim, but soon Bloomberg, CNN and finally even websites that central leaders themselves apparently kept a close eye on, like those of the *Financial Times* and the *New York Times*, were either permanently or sporadically blocked. By 2021, even the last one standing, LinkedIn, finally succumbed and withdrew its services in China.

Xi's government were willingly assisted in this great project of separation by companies like Alibaba. They had the most precious resource of all – vast amounts of data on what Chinese people were buying, what was trending, what they were interested in: a million clues as to what made them tick. A visit to Alibaba's headquarters in Hangzhou, shortly before the October congress in 2017, brought this home to me. On a screen, the presenters from the company PR department showed real-time information on how goods were moving around China, what was popular at any particular moment, who was expressing interest in what. Soon Alibaba was being pressurised by another entity, Tencent QQ, which is the Chinese equivalent of Facebook and Twitter combined. In their vast skyscraper in Shenzhen, they were also harvesting information. Entering the meeting rooms at the top of their headquarters, which I visited a year later, a huge sign declared that this private company was 'serving the party'.

Tencent and its ilk had no choice in this. In a National Intelligence Law introduced in 2017, extremely broad definitions were given to what constituted security. All the state information service Xinhua would say, when the law was passed by the National People's Congress on 27 June, was that it was an 'intelligence law to safeguard national security and interests'.[5] Foreign commentators were more damning. Calling the law 'insidious and pervasive', one writer stated that 'it does indeed oblige citizens to spy on one another – the only question is at what point in the process the spying can legally begin'.[6] The political reality was that there was no way the party would let such an opportunity pass it by. That would have undermined its claim that it was the custodian of the mission of national greatness, and therefore free to use any means to promote this endeavour. For companies to hold back this information would have been unpatriotic and treacherous. It was not only their duty, but, in the party's view, their honour to contribute this for the national good.

The mindset betrayed by this legislation was not conducive to friendly relations with the outside world, although Xi's purposeful style of governance and mode of expression created a level of predictability. By 2017, people inside and outside the country knew where China stood, whether they liked it or not. This offered an interesting conundrum. What was more unpalatable? A China that maintained a little ambiguity, one that the West could imagine converting to a state resembling democracies such as those in North America or Europe? Or a China it understood, where previous ideals would have to be set aside but at least the West would know exactly what it was up against? Had the West not demanded that China become more transparent about its aims? There were definite regulations and laws now – just not the ones the West had hoped for. What's more, the new legislation was being implemented. Companies from outside China that assumed they would receive preferential treatment, as they had in the past, found themselves rudely disabused. The playing field was flatter. China's language with the outside world was becoming blunter and less laden with polite rhetoric. Instead, it started to spell out exactly what it wanted. China's leaders had talked about a 'new normal' of slower growth from 2013. But starting in 2017, there was also a new normal in the country's geopolitics – an assertion that it now had the status and the right to be considered a great power on a par with the US. That did not mean it was *similar* to the US, nor that it planned to duplicate America's role on the global stage. Rather, it meant that it would never be spoken of as some subordinate or understudy. There was the American way, and now a Chinese way.

This new clarity on China's role meant the 2017 leadership undertook to deliver a very different message to the one the international community had invested so much in over the previous decades. In 2015, I recall one senior, retired former American National Security Advisor addressing a conference full of Chinese students from the elite Tsinghua University in Beijing, expressing his hope that, one day, 'the young people here will breathe the free air of democracy'. The applause was polite and restrained. It was a noble vision, born from good intentions. But it was also, alas, one facing a far more complex reality. For those who passionately believed that China was following the USSR and other failed Communist systems, Xi Jinping's leadership was deeply unexpected. For instance, American scholar Larry Diamond had predicted in 2012, after the Arab Spring, that a wave of democratisation would sweep across Asia, including China.[7] Historian Gordon Chang had spoken of China's imminent collapse with such regularity since 2005 that one wonders whether he hoped that, if he said it often enough, one day he would be proved right. Disappointment of figures like these (and there were many others), with a passionate and sincere commitment to the cause of democracy, was understandable – but for some, their expressions of resentment and irritation often sounded as though their feelings had got the better of them. By 2019, Diamond was saying that China's lack of meaningful democratic change posed a threat to the rest of the world.[8] The new reality would not change merely because outsiders were unhappy, as Xi made apparent when he spoke after his reappointment in 2017.

When we contemplate this more assertive, muscular tone and approach under Xi, we have to remember who his main audience is. To whom is he really speaking? In China, there exists a marginalised 1 per cent – dissidents, disaffected, haters of the system, separatists. These are figures that, rightly or wrongly, get much attention in the liberal West for their unjust treatment. Figures like the lawyer Yu Wensheng, who was imprisoned for four years in 2020 for representing contentious cases in court; or journalist Zhang Zhan, who was thrown in jail for her work exposing Covid-19 blunders by the government in 2020. These figures spread across social groups. Sun Dawu was a billionaire pig farmer whose outspoken criticism of the government was rewarded with an eighteen-year sentence in 2021. These are people who are cared about and championed outside of China. But the fact is that, within the country, they are seen by the leadership as part of the disloyal, noisy, self-centred, tiny unrepresentative minority who are soiling the country's image and causing it to lose face. Even worse, they are jeopardising the success of

China's national mission. There is no liberal doctrine of judging a society by how well it looks after its most marginalised people at work here. For the Communist Party in Beijing, the moral calculation is simple. In the New Era of national rejuvenation, disloyalty to the great message of the China Dream is a form of treason. Under Xi, the party looks after the interests of the majority, because the majority will keep the party in power. For the minority – those regarded as enemies of the system – the promises safeguarding their rights to a beautiful life do not figure. Instead, a wholly different, brutal and inhumane criterion of treatment is brought into play.

To be categorised as a person in Xi's China is to be one thing; to be a non-person is a very real, and very terrifyingly different, status that many people have. It means that your networks close in around you. People will not speak with you. Only your most immediate family will stand by your side and, sometimes, even they will abandon you. Your legal and political rights, such as they were, disappear. You lose your right to freedom of movement and association. Even a visit outside your apartment to buy food becomes a chore, as you are followed and harassed by myriad personnel from the underworld of Chinese security. In imperial times, those who lost the favour of their emperors were sent to the edges of the empire to spend their days in poverty and destitution. These days, the party cuts your internet and social media access, causing a digital, but very real, isolation. Under Xi, the China Dream is tangible for many, many people. But for a small number, it is a nightmare. That is the great moral quandary his leadership poses – whether it is acceptable to look after the interests of the vast majority with no regard for the small number of people who don't fit in.

Alongside such brittle treatment of dissidents are other significant sources of anxiety that Xi's administration must face if it is to deliver on its promises to the majority, whose support it needs to stay in power. One of the most imminent and urgent of these issues is that of demographics, that of an ageing population. Japan, South Korea and Taiwan have all come up against this issue, though with far smaller populations. In the space of a generation, family sizes have fallen from four or five children to less than one. In China, this has been exacerbated by the imposition of the one-child policy in the 1980s, which was intended to manage the country's then burgeoning population. Demographers both inside and outside China have argued about whether shrinking birth rates were caused purely by these restrictions, or whether they are due to the impact of rising wealth levels and a desire to have smaller families that kicked in even while Mao was still in control. What is certain is that China's population growth has fallen to its lowest level in six decades, the structure of the population today is one where the average age is rising and the numbers of those aged over 60 is increasing, as people have fewer children, later in their life. China's working age population has fallen to such an extent that a country that had an almost infinite supply of cheap labour a generation ago, has become one with labour shortages in manufacturing, causing wage inflation. Ageing China is a real and pressing problem, with implications for healthcare, how the elderly are looked after and pensions. Xi's government is aware of this. The family size and birthrate policy has been adapted and changed to encourage people to have more children. In 2014, married couples where both partners were single children were allowed to have two children. In 2021, even this restraint was removed to allow up to three children per couple.

What does Xi's world look like for those cadres and officials who need to implement his great project, and do something about the demographic, environmental, social and other challenges the country is facing? After all, they are the party foot soldiers, doing the most basic level work to ensure that this whole immense endeavour remains on track. The placing of Xi Jinping Thought in the constitution in 2018 was regarded as yet more evidence of the leader's hubris and arrogance. And yet, an understanding of how Xi Jinping Thought relates directly to these millions of lower-level operatives and officials is important. It is no abstract, academic matter to them but akin to a set of instructions telling them how to live.

Their performance will be assessed against this Thought, and their career success depends on delivering it. Being regarded as effective implementers will mean rising through the system, being rewarded with better jobs and greater responsibility. This is a real incentive. Chinese politics is an ultimate version of *Squid Game*, the 2021 South Korean drama, in which competitors who failed playing childhood games were immediately executed. A wrong move, a poorly made decision, a meeting where you irritate your boss or fail to keep the upper levels of government happy can have dramatic consequences. In the very worst cases, the anti-corruption enforcers can appear and turn your life upside down.

Xi complained in 2021 that officials were being too over-cautious to innovate. There are good reasons for this. On the one hand, those with even the lowest level leadership positions in Chinese towns or prefectures must remember that now, unlike in the past, their main function is to serve the people. Xi Jinping Thought places the people at the forefront of everything. But it says little about who these people are. An official will need to look after businesspeople, who generate growth and employ others; they will need to remember the many disgruntled laid-off workers and rural dwellers who feel that they are receiving none of the benefits of development gained by others; they will need to deal with petitioners, those who feel that the system has not addressed their claims for compensation and redress. Armed with the shield of Xi Jinping Thought, they will need to leave their safe government compounds and be visible, and connected, to the people. They must ensure that their public statements are in accordance with the new ideology – and that they do not slip into language that seems to support Western ideas like free markets and division of powers, or support for lawyers. Xi and his Thought have made clear, China must follow its own path.

With Xi Jinping Thought, cadres will need to support dynamic local enterprises that create the innovative Chinese companies that were made a priority in the dual circulation ideas of 2020. The days of attracting investment from foreign enterprises or trying to broker deals that allowed technology transfers with them are over. For local officials, armed with Xi Thought, the onus is on self-reliance, harking back to the years under Mao. The difference is that today the country is the world's largest exporter and second largest importer. Realising meaningful trade autonomy will not be easy. But this is what the cadres need to demonstrate they are working towards.

Then there is the final and perhaps most important issue. Success depends on doing things differently, on being a change-maker. In 2017, Xi's congress speech included a tsunami of promises – almost one full hour of his three-hour speech was about what the party needed to do next. Clean up the natural environment. Help the poor. Improve social welfare, and sort out hospitals and healthcare. Housing needed to be affordable, and of a better quality. In a country with more expensive property in some urban areas than Australia or Britain, Xi asserted in 2020 that one's house should not be an investment opportunity but a place to live. Alas, for local officials, selling off property for commercial development, no matter who the inhabitants are, is one of the few ways they have been allowed to make money. The Xi government was promising a pension system for the ageing population, and a better, world class education system. It was saying that people could have the jobs they wanted and the lifestyle they dreamt about. The party was their servant on this, and officials at the local level were on the front line of making sure this whole edifice worked.

However, the problem with doing things differently is the heightened risk of failure. For Xi, as for Deng, success is the 'sole criterion of truth'. But the much more common corollary is not great – failure is the road to perdition. A wrong initiative, an idea put into practice that goes awry, will receive no mercy. The sky can only have one sun in it. This is a law of physics and Chinese politics. And Xi alone shines. The risk of being accused of failure and the ensuing costs were why, in late 2019, when some doctors on a messaging service in the central city of Wuhan started talking of seeing patients suffering from a strange new cold, local officials silenced them. When the ophthalmologist Li Wenliang spoke of his worries about this new cold, he was told by local security officers to stop making trouble. Tragically, he died of the virus a few weeks later. For a few critical days, the Wuhan officials trusted to their luck, hoping that the problem would go away. But this time, their gamble didn't pay off. On 31 December 2019, the central government finally alerted the World Health Organization (WHO) that the virus, which was then named SARS-CoV-2, was causing Covid-19, a severe respiratory disease similar to the SARS outbreak the country had experienced almost two decades before. Spreading like wildfire, by the middle of January 2020 it was already appearing abroad. By March, the world was in the grips of a full-grown pandemic.

The officials in Wuhan were no doubt as zealous in their fidelity to Xi Jinping Thought as those elsewhere. This did not stop two senior officials from the local health bureau being sacked in early February, followed by the top official for the whole of Hubei province, Jiang Chaoliang, who went the same way a few days later. Ma Guoqiang, his counterpart in Wuhan itself, was removed the same day. Draconian lockdowns were announced wherever cases of the virus were found. Initially, the rest of the world watched from a distance, writing, as they had with SARS in 2003, of this pandemic largely being a Chinese affair. But in March, similar orders for people to work from home, wear face masks and not to socialise were issued in the UK, across Europe and in the US.

Like Mao, and Deng, Xi Jinping Thought eschews book learning; it is presented as an ideology. It is akin to a code of practice, a way of living that officials, the priests of the party faith, have to follow. Armed with this new faith, they have to embrace it not only with their words, as had been the case in the past, but with their actions. Their rewards: to see their country rise higher and higher on the world stage, in terms of the power attributed to it and the fear it generates. In early 2022, a mocking film appeared on the Xinhua website of two Chinese actors pretending to be a figure called James Pond, agent 0.07, and his assistant. They spoke of a world cowering in fear before China, that China was the heart of all their worries and the greatest security issue of the time. It was a pointed message. China might have not wanted this kind of acknowledgement in the past, but the discomfort of the FBI in the US, and MI6 in London, showed that it really mattered. For all the stress and risks from their jobs – which were often poorly paid and increasingly prone to public scrutiny and pressure – like most people serving a faith, there were rewards for the average party official under Xi. They were servants of the main objective of Xi Thought – the construction of a great, powerful nation, which had finally found its own way. This was the New Era that Xi referred to in 2017. The future had arrived. It belonged to China. Finally, victoriously, Chinese were not only masters of their own affairs, as had been promised in the past.

They were masters of more and more of the world outside. As Xi Thought said, all they had to do was believe, and this, their great dream, would come true.

CHAPTER SIX

Xi and the World – 2021 Onwards

Where does China stand in the year the Communist Party celebrates its 100th anniversary? This is a moment of historic significance, and one that Xi extracted maximum symbolic importance from in July 2021, despite the country still battling Covid-19. For all the focus on delivering domestic prosperity and a better life to all loyal Chinese citizens, China's internal affairs are also intrinsically global. When concerns about the Chinese property market falling surfaced in late 2021, they were seen as prefiguring a global recession. China generates a fifth of global GDP. As with America, when China suffers, so does the rest of the world.

Leaders of modern China since 1949 have had varying levels of experience of the outside world. Mao only managed to leave China twice in his life – both times to the USSR, and both times in a manner as though he were the younger sibling visiting a bigger brother to receive instructions. Deng Xiaoping lived in France for a number of years from the age of sixteen. During his time there, he spent a month in late 1925 working at a Renault fitting factory in Boulogne-Billancourt, near Paris. Ostensibly he was studying for the rest of his stay, but in reality he was working as a political agitator among the Chinese community. Despite reportedly liking croissants for the rest of his life, he showed no signs of speaking nor of understanding the French language. Jiang Zemin, in stark contrast, was a polyglot, with a good command of Russian, and English serviceable enough to belt out a rendition of 'Oh My Darling, Clementine' during a state banquet in London in 1999. He had lived and studied for a number of years in the Soviet Union in the 1950s. On the contrary, Hu Jintao and Xi Jinping never lived abroad. Before becoming national leader in 2012, Xi was marginally more exposed to the outside world thanks to his very brief visit to Iowa in 1985, but his trips oversees were always as part of delegations.

Despite their varying level of foreign experience, all of these leaders were committed to a vision of China and believed that the country needed to be respected and looked up to by the outside world. Each one held to a narrative that modern Chinese history was constructed on a deep sense of shame for China's victimisation by foreign powers in the early part of the 20th century, and its subsequent impoverishment following the Sino-Japanese War. Mao's revolutionary and ideological convictions meant that he saw exploitation and feudalism even deeper within Chinese society reaching far back into imperial history. This view has slowly weakened, so that today the imperial era has been reframed by Xi in a more positive and admiring light. In this way, Chinese traditional civilisation is presented as a great asset and serves as the bed-rock of national identity.

In 2022, Xi has been recast as a leader in the imperial mould; he speaks on behalf of China as though his leader-ship is not just about its own power but represents something intrinsically significant about the country and its identity to the rest of the world. He is a strong leader, the message goes, for a strong country. His language is framed so that he is portrayed as the servant of Chinese people abroad, representing the nation's collective interests and aspirations. There is nothing strange about this in itself. It is a fundamental role of any head of state. The difference for Xi is the unique status of the nation he leads, in relation to the rest of the world, which comes laden with conflicting meanings and pressures. This comes back to that ambiguous attitude mentioned earlier – the two stories of China as a mesmerising economic opportunity but with a terrible reputation for human rights. Diplomatically, the outside world views it both as a place of strong cultural inter-est and appeal, but also, in its current political form, one that alienates and frightens people. The very fact that it subscribes to a form of Communism is one reason for this. Perhaps the West's greatest weakness towards China is the ambiguity of its own attitude towards it.

By 2022, one of the points of attack towards Xi is that he is a dictator of a country that does not really exist. This line of thought suggests that the country he represents is an artificial invention, to some extent, with profound underlying potential fractures and causes of instability that will, at some point, cause the whole place to implode and break up. Bill Hayton has written of the invented status of contemporary China, and the way it has emerged from a number of different predecessor states.[1] Similar points could be made about almost every nation on the planet. But there are valid questions about how the very shrill nationalist tone in China, which has only intensified since 2012, is prompted not by outside questions like this but by an inner sense of vulnerability and doubt among Chinese people themselves. Diplomats like Zhao Lijian started to appear during the Covid-19 crisis in 2020, deploying shockingly aggressive language towards those seen as attacking China in ways that hinted at how sensitive and insecure Chinese beliefs might be.[2] Xi's brand of Communism is, in some ways, an answer to this sense of insecurity. It is very much about removing this lack of confidence and telling the Chinese they should be proud of who they are, and not to doubt their unity and coherence as a nation. But this is obviously not an easy thing to learn in a few years.

This explains why, particularly since 2017, Xi has talked strongly about how the singular, uniform party he represents also stands for the best interest of the singular, uniform country it is in charge of, guarding against this underlying fear and insecurity. Xi is insistent that the Chinese people should be proud of who they are and feel that their own culture is every bit as strong, if not stronger, than that of Americans or Europeans. He and his party make strong claims about a very distinctive, almost monolithic Chinese identity and history, which they represent and protect from threats. Party and nation are bound together so tightly in this discourse that it is sometimes hard to tell them apart. The message is, as with so much else Xi says, unambiguous. There would be no modern China without the focus and unity of the Communist Party reassuring everyone that the vexatious questions and doubts of foreigners are both insincere and wrong.

This approach does arouse strong emotions. The bottom line is that Xi Jinping Thought has proved to be profoundly nationalistic. The problem is that while nationalism might be inflamed by the party and often prove useful to it, it can also run out of the party's control. Relations with Japan are one of the important examples of this, due to the complex, often horrifying and destructive track record between the two nations in the first half of the 20th century. These matters still play a real part in politics and diplomacy today. In 2004, for instance, a final between China and Japan in the Asian Football Cup held in Beijing, in which the latter were victorious, resulted in widespread riots across the city. One report said, 'Japanese flags were burned, there were calls for boycotts of Japanese goods and boos and jeers greeted Japan's every move.'[3] Seventeen years later, things had not improved. During the 2021 Olympics held in Tokyo, there was widespread claims in China that the Japanese hosts were discriminating against Chinese participants. In events like table tennis, a sport where China has enjoyed almost total dominance since it began participating in the games after a long hiatus in 1984, a loss by two Chinese stars to their Japanese counterparts prompted enraged complaints against 'Little Japan'.[4] In an unpredictable world, it seems that continuing bad blood between these two nations is one of the very few things that one can be certain of.

If we accept that Xi Jinping is a man of faith, then at the core of that creed is a pure form of nationalism. This is a living belief system that unites the present with the past and the future and joins the heart and the mind. From 2014, Xi and his colleagues often used the word 'comprehensive'; theirs was a comprehensive leadership, undertaking comprehensive reform and seeking to implement what was called the 'Four Comprehensives'. These demanded that focus be put on building a prosperous society, improving rule of law, continuing economic reform and governing the party well. The Four Comprehensives acted as the precursor to Xi Jinping Thought. But standing over the various uses of the term, what lay at the heart of them was the comprehensive construction of a great Chinese state. Nationalistic fidelity to this is one of the strongest threads linking Xi with former leaders, with his current colleagues and with the country's citizens. In a world of fragmentation and disunity, such an explicit faith gives the party the most precious of all assets – a united, uncomplicated message, which everyone in the country can believe in, despite their differences. In my observation from 1991 when I started dealing with China, it was often the Chinese who were accused by the West of not having a real, coherent set of beliefs or vision, which meant that they could continue the anomaly of practising capitalism economically while maintaining a Communist system. Now, with the US politically divided, and Europe mired down with in-fighting until the tragic invasion of Ukraine by Russia in February 2022 caused signs of a new sense of unity and purpose – the durability of which is hard to confidently predict at the time of writing – China is a place of true faith.

The role of Covid-19 between 2020 and 2022 illustrates this tale of two convictions – China and its nationalist faith versus the West and its self-defeating love of pluralism and uninhibited but undefined freedom. The crisis originally looked as though it might envelop China, but by mid-2020, it had exposed almost every other form of governance to be inadequate and wanting, showing how misjudged the original criticisms levelled at China had been. As noted earlier, China had experienced significantly lower rates of infection and fatalities than Europe or America. While the Chinese data may be an underestimate, it would need to be either a colossal act of miscounting or a huge concerted effort to downplay the extent of the infections for the real figure to reach the same levels seen in America and Europe. It was not surprising that the Beijing government used this as a propaganda opportunity and a testament to the viability of their own system. To Xi and his colleagues it was tangible proof that, in democracies, people are so wedded to the notion of individual freedom that they prioritised it at the cost of their own health.

Covid-19 has provided the fuel by which Chinese nationalism has been turbo-charged. The Chinese looked at how their government had managed to control the spread of the virus, and then at the staggering statistics produced by countries as far afield as Australia, the UK, Italy and Canada, and shook their heads in astonishment. Here was positive proof that socialism with Chinese characteristics could perform better than Western capitalism – as long as the country had faith.

Covid-19 also proved to be an international crisis laden with geopolitical symbolism and meaning. It has confirmed all the fears that the US and China in particular have about each other. By mid-2020, Xi announced the idea of 'dual circulation'. In many ways, this was a reflection of what was already taking place – the attempt to decouple the Chinese domestic market with its rising middle-class consumers from the outside world, and to give them a stronger role in fuelling growth. In the past, China manufactured goods to export to the outside world. Zhu Rongji, premier in the late 1990s, called the country the factory of the world. One plant produced most of the world's microwave ovens, while another made a large proportion of its socks. But by Xi's second term in power, this was no longer the economic model his government wanted. Instead, it wished to have innovative, technologically strong home brands. That prompted the 'Made in China 2025' campaign that so riled the Americans during Trump's presidency. Trump's response to the campaign was that China was a free-loading cheat, a country to which the US had extended the hand of friendship and concord in the 1980s and 1990s and which was, by the late 2010s, a systemic competitor, an ideological opponent with its Communist system and a threat. In 2021, former US Vice-President Mike Pence typified this stance, saying that 'Communist China' posed 'a greater challenge to the United States than the Soviet Union ever did throughout the Cold War'.[5] For Chinese nationalists, this was high praise indeed.

Under Xi, China is confidently facing the world as never before. No other Chinese leader has ever travelled so extensively while in power. His start in 2013 was orthodox, visiting Russia as Hu had done for his initial overseas visit a decade before. But from that point, Xi's air miles have rocketed. He has visited countries in the Australasian region, from Indonesia to Australia, some of them multiple times. He has made several visits to Latin America, historically a place of lower Chinese involvement because of the number of allies recognising the Republic of China on Taiwan (created after the Chinese Civil War in 1949, when the defeated Nationalists under Chiang Kai-shek fled to the island to continue their regime there), rather than the People's Republic. He went to Europe, enjoying a trip to the UK in late 2015 where he quaffed a pint of bitter in a British pub with the then Prime Minister David Cameron and presided over a subsequently much-mocked rebranding of UK–China relations as being in a 'golden age'. In 2014, he became the first leader of China to speak at the headquarters of the European Union in Brussels. He went to various countries in Africa and undertook a tour through the Middle East to Egypt and Saudi Arabia in 2016. Countries big and small received his attention. In 2015, he declared during a speech in Seattle that despite all the speculation about internal power struggles and dramatic in-fighting in his administration, 'there was no *House of Cards*' in Beijing politics, a reference to the popular political thriller, which depicted the Machiavellian plans of an ambitious and almost pathologically ruthless American politician.[6]

Before Covid-19 halted international travel, Xi had visited over 65 countries. He also attended multilateral forums, from the UN to the World Economic Forum in Davos in early 2017 – another first for a Chinese head of state. China also hosted events like the 2016 G20 summit in Hangzhou. In all of these, the Xi leadership used language and references tailored to the audiences that he was addressing. When overseas, there were copious references to the literature and culture of the host country. In Russia, that meant a long list of Russian novelists from Tolstoy to Gorky, Dostoyevsky to Gogol. In Britain, it meant quoting Shakespeare. In Germany, it was all about Goethe. Sometimes he referenced historic events or famous sites. The tone was always one of respect, inviting reciprocal recognition, setting the cultural achievements of the country he was visiting alongside those of China. Friendship and common interests were stressed. As Xi stated in France in 2014, the world did not need to fear his country; his follow-up statement describing that although China was a lion, it was a 'friendly, lovely' one did not come across as reassuring as was perhaps intended.

The enormous amount of time and effort expended on this diplomacy shows how committed Xi is to promoting China's image and ensuring that its interests are represented on the world stage. In the past, many commentators and policy makers in the West had generally assumed that Chinese leaders' overwhelming interests and greatest challenges were within the country, and that international matters were a lower priority. A vivid illustration of this was the fact that in the latter part of the Hu administration, more was frequently spent on domestic security than on national defence.[7] But under Xi, there has been a recalibration. Internal and external affairs cannot be separated. For him, going abroad is merely an extension of attending to domestic business. With rising levels of investment, trade and cooperation, and with global issues such as climate change becoming more urgent, the boundaries of Chinese interests have stretched further and further outside the country's borders. Today, the Xi era can best be described as one marked by more proactive relations with the outside world, more direct communication, the removal of ambiguities in terms of how China regards its global position and the clearer statement of national interests.

There are three areas that China regards as having direct strategic importance: the South China Sea, Hong Kong and Taiwan. They are where domestic nationalism most impacts on global affairs. From 2014, in a series of startling moves, China started to build permanent structures on rock formations in the South China Sea, meaning that they could be classified as islands and strengthen its role in the region against contending powers who also have claims there, such as Vietnam, the Philippines and Malaysia. It constructed runways on some of them, even though these places could barely accommodate a single house. Coupled with its vast army, these islands meant that China was able to exercise a wholly new kind of power in its region. Historically, China had been a land, not a sea power. Under Xi, its transformation into a 'comprehensive' power has been completed. Once it dreamt of ruling the waves; now, as never before, in the Asia Pacific it has the chance to do so.

Xi's nationalism has been equally apparent when it comes to Hong Kong. The city had little democracy until the final few years of British colonial rule, when the last governor, British politician Chris Patten, brought in modest electoral reforms – much to the fury of Beijing. When the city was handed back to Chinese sovereignty in 1997, it was promised a large degree of autonomy, for 50 years at least. Even before Xi, there were rising concerns about the city's identity, with larger and larger numbers of mainland visitors and increasing signs of control and potential interference. In 2014, however, proposals to change how Hong Kong elected its chief executive brought out a large number of protestors. The central district of the city was occupied. Beijing angrily denounced what it called riots provoked by outside agents. More protests against mainland China's interference in Hong Kong continued into 2017. Xi's visit to mark the twentieth anniversary of the handover that year led to a curt statement that Hong Kong would toe the line – and that chaotic demonstrations by pro-democracy forces were against the national interest. Since that time, space for dissent and assertion of the city's uniqueness have dried up altogether. With the passing of a national security law in 2020, imposed by Beijing and containing very broad definitions of what might be constituted as disruptive behaviour, control tightened even further. For Xi and his colleagues, the message is simple: Hong Kong is, to use his phrase from 2017, regarded as wholly Chinese, where Chinese affairs can only be decided by the Chinese. Nationalism prevails here. Outsiders are not welcome to interject in this space. The commentary and search for influence by British and other interested parties was greeted with a rejection that was almost brutal in its disdain and indifference. In November 2020, the Five Eyes alliance in intelligence sharing – the US, Canada, New Zealand, the UK and Australia – criticised Chinese policy in Hong Kong; in response, China's most aggressive (and domestically most popular) Ministry of Foreign Affairs spokesperson Zhao Lijian stated, 'No matter if they have five eyes or ten eyes, if they dare to harm China's sovereignty, security and development interests, they should beware of their eyes being poked and blinded.'[8]

But of all these issues, it is the final one, Taiwan, where Xi may hope to claim his place in history. Enjoying de facto independence since 1949, in the early days of Xi's presidency, a conciliatory stance was adopted towards the island that lies only 160 kilometres from the People's Republic's southern coast. The status quo was maintained, where both sides asserted there was but one true China, but neither accepted the other's definition of what constituted this China. This ambiguity meant that in 2015, in Singapore, the respective leaders of the two places could actually meet for the first time since 1945. Taiwan's President Ma Ying-jeou and Xi enjoyed a meal together, and courteously addressed each other as 'Mr Ma' and 'Mr Xi', to avoid any unpleasantness about the other's legitimacy. Ma was seen as keen on maintaining links with Beijing. But Xi is the great disambiguator. When Ma's replacement, Tsai Ing-wen, was elected, the time for assertion arrived. Although she was a pragmatist, she came from a party with far stronger leanings towards outright independence; Beijing is violently opposed to this and has consistently said that it would respond to any moves in this direction with military action. Elected in 2016, and re-elected in 2020, Tsai has witnessed the negative impact of the repressive measures on Hong Kong. The use of the 'one country, two systems' model, whereby Hong Kong was reintegrated back into the mainland from 1997, now holds almost no appeal for Taiwan.

With Tsai in power, China started to eradicate any space for ambiguity in which people could engage with both sides without spelling out their position on the island's sovereignty and Beijing's claims to it. China has put pressure on the few countries still recognising Taiwan as an independent state, managing to persuade Panama, a long-standing ally of Taipei, to swap sides in 2017, and Nicaragua to do the same in 2021. China also started to be far more muscular in its international approaches, speaking forcefully and angrily when then president-elect Trump had a brief phone conversation with Tsai in late 2016, becoming the first US leader to speak directly to a Taiwanese premier since the late 1970s when America still recognised Taiwan diplomatically.

Taiwan is the place where Chinese nationalism could get scariest. Escalation of military exercises and aggressive air drills very close to the island's airspace, and sometimes encroaching on it, aroused claims of bullying in 2022. A 2014 comment Xi made to a visiting Taiwanese dignitary implied that this was not an issue that he felt could be kicked down the road indefinitely. After all, in his view the country had been separated since 1949, a situation that should never have persisted for so many decades; the regions were meant to be inextricably welded to each other. This was in the face of arguments by historians that Taiwan had only been a part of China proper for the four brief years following Japan's defeat in 1945.* At some point a political resolution would be neces-

---

* Prior to that, since 1895, the island was under Japanese control, and before that had a complex relationship with various earlier Chinese

sary, Xi demanded. Increasingly, Americans and others have talked of this issue being the potential catalyst for a full-blown war between the two superpowers. For the Xi leadership, with its sense of historic importance and mission, this is indeed the one matter where it should be able secure its reputation as the great nationalist defender of a unified China.

Such a war, were it ever to happen, would be not only a regional but a global catastrophe. For Taiwan's 23 million inhabitants, who have a strong sense of their own national identity, it would be an event that is absolutely imposed on them against their will.[9] For the US and its allies, it would be a direct, aggressive attack on a fellow democracy which they would most likely feel morally and legally obliged to defend. For China, the move would pose vast challenges about how, even if their military actions were successful in physically taking the island, they would be able to govern 23 million people who would not accept their rule. Taiwan is the greatest issue where the creed of Chinese nationalism and its heightened emotions and zealous commitment might bring the country directly into conflict with the outside world. Meanwhile, the party watches for opportunity, and continues to probe and test, waiting perhaps for the time when all of this might wear down

---

dynasties. In the 17th century it was also very briefly both a Dutch and Spanish colony.

the nerves of both Taiwanese and the outside world and bring about capitulation. They might be in for a long wait.

The other great geopolitical issue Xi faces is that of international criticism of actions in its western border areas, Tibet and Xinjiang being the most contentious. Until recently, the Tibetan issue enjoyed the higher international profile. This is in no small part due to the Dalai Lama, who fled from the capital Lhasa to India when China annexed the region in 1959. Since then, he has been a tireless figurehead promoting the Tibetan cause, winning the Nobel Peace Prize in 1989. From India, the Tibetan government-in-exile has worked to promote the autonomy of their homeland. Sporadic dialogue with the Chinese government has so far led nowhere. Historians argue about the status of Tibet; however close the link between Tibet and different Chinese imperial dynasties, this was in the era long before notions of sovereignty were accepted in this region, and therefore hard to describe accurately in modern terminology. A number of protests occurred in the 1980s, culminating in a major uprising in 2008, before the Beijing Olympics. This was a particularly sensitive moment for Beijing's leaders in view of the heightened attention being paid to their country at the time. Since then, protests have taken the form of self-immolations, largely by Buddhist monks but sometimes by secular activists. From 2009, there have been 155 acts of self-immolation, which has led to 133 deaths, and this has prompted claims of Chinese government repression against religious institutions.[10]* From 2013, an intense security campaign led to the reduction and then almost complete eradication of these acts on Chinese soil, but at a huge cost to whatever freedoms the local people had. The Chinese government's argument has consistently been that it wishes to see Tibet develop economically, and that any religious or cultural practices that are not disloyal to the state are allowed. In reality, the parameters of what is considered threatening are drawn, often arbitrarily and capriciously, very wide. Economic development has indeed taken place, with Tibet still the recipient of large amounts of central government subsidies and subventions, but the region remains relatively impoverished, with good evidence that government support tends to go to settlers from outside, most of whom are from the Han ethnic group.

Xinjiang presents even more complex issues. The vast area of the autonomous region amounts to almost a sixth of the whole country's landmass. It has, officially at least, over 40 ethnic minority groups. The Turkic Uyghur, many of whom practise Islam, are the largest of these, making up 45 per cent of the population today. Strategically, Xinjiang occupies a great

---

* This is despite the fact that Xi, according to rumour, once had a sympathetic interest in Buddhism. His wife has even been accused of being a practitioner. There is no evidence whatsoever of any sympathy towards this area by his administration.

geographical and geopolitical crossroads. Bordering Russia, Mongolia and the gateway to Central Asia, historically, it was the main route for the various trade pathways through to the Middle East and Europe. With a long, torturous history, it was assimilated into the Qing empire in the mid-17th century. In the middle of the 20th century, a part of the area was an independent country for a few years. An agreement with the USSR meant that it was assimilated into the new People's Republic in 1949. Until the start of the 21st century it was a place of perpetual, but largely low-profile, restiveness. Various groups agitated for either meaningful autonomy or outright independence. The whole context for the protests changed with the 11 September 2001 terrorist attacks in the US. China became as married to the idea of a global war on terror as the Bush presidency in Washington. Briefly, it even figured as an ally with the West. Its main fear was that the sort of terrorist campaigns fuelled by militant Islam in Afghanistan, Pakistan and elsewhere in Central Asia would start to creep into China. With the Kunming train station attack of 2014, the new Xi administration grew convinced that its worst fears were about to be realised. Its implementation of hugely expensive, widespread and repressive measures from 2017 were carefully documented through the analysis of satellite images that showed extensive internment centres being built. Many investigations, such as the Uyghur Tribunal held in London, which delivered its judgment in 2021, argued that this was a campaign of genocidal proportions. However, the judgment issued by the tribunal was careful to clarify the ways in which they were using this term, and the fact that they had not uncovered evidence of mass killings but of human rights abuses and suppression of culture.[11] There has also been condemnation by governments and parliaments, such as those of Canada, the UK and Germany. The impact of this issue on international opinion has been huge, and a disaster for China's global image. It has been used by those campaigning against the Chinese government as the main reason why it is unfit to be trusted and why it should be ostracised, struggled against and, one day, felled.

Xi's government has shown its desire to craft more communicative and positive messages to engage with the outside world and an awareness that constructive dialogue is hugely important. However, as of February 2022, consistent, widespread and sustained international criticism from the US, Europe and others regarding China's behaviour in the South and East China Seas, Hong Kong, Taiwan, Tibet and, in particular, Xinjiang have resulted in no backing down by the Beijing government. Xi smiles at the world, but his policy remains unchanged on these principal areas, even though life on the international stage might be much easier were he to do so. This has caused intense speculation. Is this because, despite his outwards showing of strength, he is incapable of causing a fundamental change in these areas? Or is it because, behind the mask of appearing to engage with the world, he is a tyrant who harbours racial disdain against any but his own Han ethnic group?

In Chinese eyes, there has been a decline of moral authority and political competence by players like the US, the European Union and others, and rising faith in their own nationalism. With regard to Xinjiang, Xi and his colleagues can plot a line from the messy and unsuccessful series of interventions made over the past twenty years in the Middle East by the US and others, and the terrorist attacks in Europe and America that have happened in the same period. This by no means justifies the actions the Chinese government has undertaken. But it does help to explain them. The fact is that had the West been more successful in its handling of terrorism, it would have more authority to show China that there are better alternatives to managing potential security threats than outright suppression. Instead, the one thing that might have changed Chinese behaviour in places like Xinjiang – policies and measures that the West could show China demonstrably improved security – were lacking. Never have Washington, London and Brussels needed to speak more urgently and powerfully about Chinese actions and been heard. But in 2022, they have never been more discredited nor looked more impotent and irrelevant. Instead, Beijing has the sense that Western motives are purely to contain China's success. That is not merely the West's tragedy, but a tragedy for the people in Xinjiang and beyond.

Xi's efforts since 2012 to create a series of new frameworks by which China could relate to the outside world as a global power, but one with Chinese characteristics, have resulted in the creation of a number of slogans and phrases. These explain China's view of its role, and the relations it has with the wider world. The original slogan was the 'China Dream', which, on its first outing in early 2012 was declared to be something that anyone could have, not only Chinese people. From this flowed related stories about China's relations with particular regions and counties. The meta-narrative was in place. Now came the detail. All of these micro-stories insisted on reciprocity and parity between China and whichever other nation or region was being discussed. In 2013, while in America to meet President Obama, Xi announced that their bilateral relations offered a 'new model for major powers'. Although he did not spell it out, it was obvious that only the US and his country needed to be considered in this New Era.

For Europe, Xi's language referred to partner civilisations. Speaking in Bruges in 2014, Xi flattered the Europeans by referring to their rich cultural achievements and their high levels of development over the centuries. Underneath this was the more prosaic reality that for China, while Europe figured as an intellectual partner, with strong universities and excellent tourist resources and a major consumer market, it did not register in terms of hard power. Seeing the diverse countries of Europe as a single civilisational entity meant the continent had only one story, rather than many. This approach also meant that as civilisations, there was no question of hierarchy, or of who was superior. Europe and China were equals in terms of the glorious cultural achievements from their pasts and their contribution to humankind.

For the immense complexity of China's land neighbours, and its maritime area, everything was linked to the New Silk Road, which transformed over 2014 into the One Belt One Road, until finally being labelled the Belt and Road Initiative (BRI) a year later. These three different names represented one thing – something akin to a vast free trade zone centred on China, embracing more than 80 countries regionally and across the globe, where it intended to sell its goods and trade. This is Xi foreign policy par excellence. It allows China to apply the knowledge it has acquired over the decades since the economic reforms of the early 1980s to the service of the many other countries looking for ways to emulate parts of its success. The BRI has been exhaustively commented on. Countering China's claims that the initiative is purely about reciprocity and material improvement, there has been widespread coverage of more negative accusations: that it is self-centred, focussing on exporting Chinese labour, promoting debt traps and creating even more political leverage over developing countries. Hambantota International Port in Sri Lanka is a high profile example. Originally expanded in 2012, with loans from a Chinese state-owned bank, by 2017, spiralling debts meant that 85 per cent of the project was sold to China Merchants Group on a 99-year lease. This sort of deal was labelled 'debt trap diplomacy', because China was often the only viable partner, and the country was accused of extracting maximum returns and gaining strategically important investments such as ports.[12] For the most optimistic, the BRI is akin to the Marshall Plan, the US-led aid scheme that successfully rebuilt Europe after the Second World War. But to its critics, the BRI is nothing more than a means to deliver a *Pax Sinica*, geared up to rope countries in to China's agenda. By this metric, using entities like the Silk Road Fund and the Asian Infrastructure Investment Bank, established in 2015 at the instigation of China, Xi's country has created a global shadow system to subvert and ultimately replace the US-led order with its alliance system, the use of the US dollar as the main international currency and US military dominance.

Xi's political investment in the idea of the BRI is clear. It was written into the state constitution in 2017, demonstrating its permanence and high status. It shows that a country in China's position should and does have global vision, confirming the nationalist narrative that the country is now truly a global player. Whatever questions remain about its true aims, the BRI spells out the sheer extent of China's ambitions for a greater role in world affairs.

China has also created narratives with a more global nature, particularly the idea of a common destiny for humanity. Since 2014, this has been used to emphasise the role that the country plays, and is willing to play, in resolving global conflicts and issues. Climate change is the most potent of these. There are many questions about how China frames this question, and how realistic its challenging targets for reducing and eliminating carbon emissions are. But there is no doubt about the ways in which the country has taken ownership over dealing with this issue since 2012, even if only for its own benefit. But how likely is it that this approach will be effective in garnering support from outsiders? Few of those angered by Chinese behaviour in Xinjiang, Hong Kong, Taiwan or the South China Sea are likely to be reassured on hearing of the country's willingness to work on solving longer-term goals that might relate to the outside world, such as climate change or dealing with pandemics. As former president of the Maldives, Mohamed Nasheed, said at the COP26 international conference on climate change held in Glasgow in late 2021, disappointed by China's refusal to set out more ambitious reductions on use of fossil fuels, 'If you want to be world leaders, this is an issue that you have to embrace and you have to lead. It is difficult to think how other countries now can think China is a leader.'[13]

Until 2016, the newness of the Xi leadership, and the distractions caused by the crisis in the Middle East and Russia's annexation of Crimea, meant that those China-originated narratives exposing a more proactive and communicative foreign policy position were launched to a largely muted response from the rest of the world. The US was unhappy about some aspects of the BRI. But the core issues of the South China Sea, Hong Kong, Xinjiang and Taiwan had yet to reach a critical point of intensity. But in 2016, a constellation of issues forced China's foreign policy into a new phase. Much of this was to do with the newly elected President of the United States Donald Trump. One of his few consistent viewpoints had been about the evils of trade imbalances. China's massive surplus of exports to America consumed his interest, almost to the point of obsession. He declared that China had gamed and abused American generosity and openness through running surpluses, resulting in damage to the American job market. Between 2017 and 2019, he made a series of aggressive moves, with China increasingly represented as an overt threat to American interests. In September 2019, shortly before a further round of trade talks between the two countries, Trump declared that China was 'a threat to the world in a sense, because they're building a military faster than anybody'.[14] He had visited China in late 2017. The atmosphere seemed positive, despite the dramatic language that had preceded his trip. Oddly, Trump personally seemed to have little interest in the promotion of American values per se. His was a very transactional view: he wanted a better economic deal with Beijing. Perhaps this deployment of sheer material self-interest rather than the tone China was used to from America, where values had historically taken precedence, was what initially most unsettled Xi's chief advisers, including his main economics counsellor, Liu He. The US imposed tariffs on a swathe of Chinese goods in 2018. China responded in kind. The term 'trade war' was used by the media. Its endpoint was a deal that was agreed in January 2020. This saw marginally more generous access for US companies in the Chinese domestic services market and more protection for intellectual property rights. However, both of these clearly suited China's current stage of development, as it sought more services for its rising middle class and protection for its own intellectual property. Trump's temporary withdrawal of his country from the Paris Agreement on climate change exacerbated bilateral strains. His Vice-President Mike Pence and the combative Secretary of State Mike Pompeo increased the pressure by using extremely confrontational language, claiming it was a direct, overt, almost existential threat to the US. Chinese companies like Huawei and platforms like TikTok were barred from much of the US economy. In concert with this, Trump made it clear, despite his own lack of fondness for multilateralism, that in this area he expected solidarity from other US allies. The world had a choice – an asymmetrical relationship where either the US was demanding loyalty and obedience, or China was.

Despite this aggression, there were ways in which the Trump leadership suited Xi. Trump and he were similar in one regard – they both disliked ambiguity. Much as China might once have been regarded as a potential liberal political reformer until Xi removed the illusion, Trump made it clear that the US saw China as a threat and now dropped the more ameliorative and placatory language. This exposed real barriers between the two, which had sometimes lain submerged under vague but friendly rhetoric. Gone were the illusions of the past, that the two might one day be able to mutually change each other in a positive way. Trump disabused Americans, on behalf of China, of the idea that economic engagement was about anything other than material self-interest; it would not serve as an indirect means of political transformation. Beyond this, Trump and his circle's fixation on China as the key problem was a backhanded affirmation that the country was truly in the ascendant. Xi had managed to achieve something his predecessors had failed to – even Mao. He had inspired American fear.

The onset of the Covid-19 pandemic has posed a set of issues for Chinese diplomacy, the outcome of which are hard to predict. A potentially very dangerous time has begun. China's relations with much of the world have dramatically deteriorated. Anger has intensified over Xinjiang and Hong Kong. A narrative of Chinese malign influence and harmful intent has been created and embedded in Western consciousness. European and North American public opinion has tended to shift from an uneasy indifference to a far more widespread sense of antagonism, which can be seen in places as far afield as Australia, Japan, Britain and Canada. China's diplomacy has been shrill and counter-productive in response, with so-called 'wolf warriors', such as the spokesperson for the Ministry of Foreign Affairs Zhao Lijian, unleashed on social media, producing language as offensive and intemperate as that of online trolls and stalkers. Xi's more high-minded insistence that China stands for global cooperation and help, such as he displayed when speaking at the Davos summit in early 2017, has been accused of being empty and hypocritical. Covid-19 has had many profound impacts on our world. Of these, the shifting view on China's role in the world and its global position is among the most dramatic. China's story is more complex and harder to tell than ever before.

This portends a difficult global future. The EU, US and others are very aware of the complex situation they now face. They well know that the challenge posed by China will not be solved by wishing the country away. For important economic, climatic and other issues it is also an irrevocable partner in addressing and hopefully one day solving these issues. If its economy continues to grow, while other developed economies continue to suffer recessionary influences in the aftermath of the pandemic, China's influence will be even stronger. The framework of 'competitor, collaborator and adversary' has been deployed to try to capture this uneasy, un-straightforward situation that China is in. But China does not accept this tripartite view of itself. Xi's responses were not comforting. Despite assuring listeners in June 2021 that China remained a friend and an ally to the West, and did not seek global hegemony in any shape or form, the primacy of assertion and control as the best means of protecting China's interests became apparent in the words Xi stated during the celebrations of the 100th anniversary of the Communist Party the following month. There, he said starkly that anyone picking fights with China would 'suffer broken heads and bloodshed'.[15] It was a fitting way of performing before the organisation that means most to him – the Communist Party of China. But for the other audience – the rest of the world – it struck an ominous note and showed that nationalism on Chinese terms would be a bitter pill to swallow.

CHAPTER SEVEN

Xi and the Future

The streets leading towards the museum are quiet, even in a city like Shanghai which is perpetually in movement. Walking there, you cross the People's Park at the centre of the main administrative area. Then you go into more narrow streets, following the signposts to your destination. When you finally find the location of the First National Congress of the Communist Party, it is an unremarkable building. Its significance comes purely from what happened there over a few days in early July 1921, when a handful of individuals assembled to hold what was then classified as an illegal meeting. One of them was Mao Zedong. They were holding the first ever formal event in China of a movement inspired by the 1917 Russian Revolution, which was largely being bankrolled and supported by Moscow. As a sign of this, one of those present was a Russian activist. Another was a Dutch revolutionary. It is unclear how this hybrid group managed to communicate with each other, as there is no evidence that the foreigners spoke a word of Chinese, nor that any of the Chinese spoke much Russian or Dutch.

Standing in this building when I visited it in 2009 was a strangely moving experience. This was not because of any ideological affinity. I hadn't come here as a member of the small number of Maoist or Communist parties operating in Britain. It was the awareness of the price that would be paid by those who had spent nine days planning, dreaming and hoping back in 1921. Over the next three decades, they would go through searing experiences. At least four of them – Li Hanjun, Chen Tanqiu, Chen Gongbo and the Dutchman, Henk Sneevliet – were executed in the ensuing decades; He Shuheng was killed fighting the Nationalists in 1935; Zhou Fohai died in prison after the end of the Second World War; Zhang Guotao fled to Canada and died there in the late 1970s, an exile. Only Mao and Dong Biwu would prosper in the years ahead, and make it into old age, still Chinese Communists, and still in power. To be a Communist at the start of the movement in China may have been a glorious thing, I reflected that day, looking at the separate photos of these individuals placed in the museum display, but it was not a good choice if one wanted a long, healthy, peaceful life.

In late October 2017, almost as soon as Xi Jinping and his newly appointed senior colleagues on the Politburo Standing

Committee were in place, they proceeded to this same, heavily symbolic place. Saluting the hammer and sickle symbol of their party, which hung prominently on the walls, they swore their oath. 'It is my will to join the Communist Party of China,' they all intoned, following Xi's lead, 'uphold the party's programme, observe the provisions of the party constitution, fulfil a party member's duties, carry out the party's decisions, strictly observe party discipline, guard party secrets, be loyal to the party, work hard, fight for Communism throughout my life, be ready at all times to sacrifice my all for the party and the people, and never betray the party.' After declaring their faith, they headed off back into the outside world. They had declared the start of the New Era; now it was time to build it.

Communists like Xi Jinping adhere to an optimistic creed. Communism is, at heart, a utopian faith. According to its teachings, after the struggle, all shall be well. This sense of the bright future, visible even through the turmoil and dimness of the present, pervades much of Xi's language. Announcing the start of the new year in 2022, in his traditional 1 January address, Xi declared that 'to realise the great rejuvenation of the Chinese nation will be no easy task, like a walk in the park; it will not happen overnight, or through sheer fanfare. We must always keep a long-term perspective, remain mindful of potential risks, maintain strategic focus and determination, and "attain to the broad and great while addressing the delicate and minute".'[1] But he went on: 'The hard work and dedication of countless unsung heroes have all added to the great momentum of China's march forward in the New Era... All the sons and daughters of the Chinese nation will join forces to create a brighter future for our nation.' Earlier in his time in office, Xi had even given a timetable for the arrival of better days, setting out two 100-year goals. The longer term one was to celebrate the 100th anniversary of the country Mao Zedong had founded in 2049, when the People's Republic would be able to enjoy, in Xi's words, 'democracy with Chinese characteristics'. By 2021, the shorter term goal had been achieved – the centenary of the founding of the Communist Party, which was held that year in Beijing in July. To show just how inextricably the past, the present and the future are entwined in the mindset of contemporary Chinese leaders, an historic resolution was issued during a major party meeting, a few months later in October 2021, to add icing to the celebratory cake. This was the first such formal summation of history since 1981, when a similar statement had prepared the way for the Deng era reforms, underlining the significance of the occasion; and Mao's era had started in 1945, with the first of these resolutions.

Xi is a storyteller. That point has already been made clear. One of the most important stories he has been telling over the past decade is that of the party itself, and of its meaning in

Chinese life and the country's destiny. The year it marked the centenary of its founding was an opportunity to use the party's track record as a claim to the future. Tellingly, much of the October 2021 document was indeed about that future. Even more tellingly, while much was made of how many times it contained Xi's name (7) compared to that of Mao or any of his other predecessors, the 'party' made over 450 appearances.[2] As ever, Xi is the lead actor, but the party is the star attraction.

The document recognised that the path followed since 1949 had not been easy. While there were no explicit accounts of the vast famines in the early 1960s that led to as many as 50 million perishing, nor much on the Cultural Revolution which traumatised the party and created conditions close to civil war in the country, the story really started to bite when it reached events that took place in 1978. Based on the knowledge of what worked and what did not, accrued over the previous three decades in power, from 1980, leaders were able to create a hybrid, bespoke form of economic development and governance. The new slogans were 'practice is the sole criterion for truth' and 'liberate thinking'. In order to allow people to live materially better lives, setting up enterprises and doing business were permitted. This was not an admission of the party's previous errors. Far from it. It was proof that the party was a learning community, one whose fundamental faith in the great Chinese nation had never swayed. Although leaders since the 1980s had engaged in this epic historic mission and were the architects who built the foundations of the New Era, the mission was now reaching its apogee in the time of Xi. In 1949, the average life expectancy for a Chinese man was 36, and per capita GDP was less than India's. But in early 2020, with great fanfare and symbolic importance, China was able to announce that absolute poverty had been eradicated, and that it was not the youthfulness of its population that was the main problem, but their ever-increasing age. For Chinese people, living in newly built cities, driving locally manufactured, well-made cars, working in good quality, service sector jobs, able to send their children to universities that now ranked among the world's best, the China Dream had arrived as fast as one of the high-speed trains rocketing across the country.

A number of promises made by the party in 2021 hinted at what the future might look like for China. The year 2035 was highlighted as a significant moment, a landmark on the way to modernity with Chinese characteristics. New heights will be reached in every dimension of material, political, cultural-ethical, social and ecological advancement, the 2021 resolution promised. Modernisation of China's system and capacity for governance will be achieved. China will consolidate its role as a global leader in terms of national strength and international influence. The inequalities that have blighted the country's growth model in recent decades will be addressed, resulting in prosperity for all. As a result of this, the Chinese people will enjoy happier, safer and healthier lives. Finally, the Chinese nation will stand taller and prouder among the nations of the world.[3]

But what does this grand-sounding language mean in practice for Chinese people? Despite the lack of official survey data about what their priorities might be, it's obvious that the Chinese government needs to ensure it keeps the majority of its citizens onside, poring obsessively over online data to find out what they want. Behind the slightly unsettling language of Communist politics, domestic bread-and-butter issues in China look little different to elsewhere. Housing and living costs continue to rise. In 2021, the persistent defaulting of major Chinese property developer Evergrande raised the spectre of the Chinese housing market collapsing once more, underlining how absolutely critical this sector is for the country. According to Chinese government data, since 1999 the annual average increase in house prices was 8 per cent year on year.[4] Over the same period, the annual average wage rose about 2.5 times, from 40,000 Chinese yuan (about $6,300 at the time of writing) to 97,000 Chinese yuan (about $15,300). As in other countries, property has become a new source of wealth; it is also more and more expensive, moving away from what people can actually afford, with some of the country's most successful entrepreneurs making money in real estate and development.

Huge new apartment blocks have been constructed in major Chinese cities. Beijing is a good case study. At the turn of the millennium, the capital had 10.3 million people. By 2022, this had risen to 21.3 million, with a projection of a further 4 million due to move there in the coming decade.[5] Between 2003 and 2014, Chinese builders created 5.5 million new apartments a year, far more than any other country in the world, most of them in urban areas or areas becoming urban.[6] But although this construction has been a source of enrichment, it is also a source of potential impoverishment. Since the mid-2000s it has been predicted that the bubble will burst on this immense economic asset. By 2016, a modest-sized 90 square metre apartment in Beijing or Shanghai fetched 25 times the average annual household income, meaning that those individuals buying these properties became slaves to debt and mortgage repayments.[7] Communist system or not, the average Chinese person is beset by the same constant pressures to pay their mortgage and try to maintain their standard of living as those in Europe or North America. Like people everywhere, their greatest economic asset is often the place they live in. For the Xi leadership, ensuring that people's wages are high enough to make their mortgage repayments is a top priority. Creating new jobs for 9 million university students who graduate each year is one important way of doing this – as acknowledged in the delayed 2020 National People's Congress, which looked at rising urban unemployment and underemployment and committed to addressing both. But will this be enough?

It is not only worries over bricks and mortar and earning enough to live that prey on the minds of the average Chinese person. Health and welfare is crucial too. By 2019, life expectancy was 74 years for a man and 79 years for women, bringing the country almost on a par with other developed countries like the UK and the US.[8] Major campaigns to encourage healthier lifestyles by cutting down on drinking and smoking have been complicated by the large rise in eating meat and increased obesity in the country. Infectious diseases have been big issues for China in the recent past. By 2020, the greatest causes of death were exactly the same as those in the West – heart disease and cancer. In the same year, 5.3 per cent of China's GDP was spent on healthcare, compared to 9.9 per cent in the UK and 16.8 per cent in the US.[9] To address future health needs for its population, China's health system will need dramatic reform and far more resources. Hospitals, which at present have highly variable levels of quality of treatment, are the main point of contact for patients. A basic national healthcare insurance system is in place but, for many, payment for treatment remains the norm. Those unfortunate enough to suffer from chronic illnesses requiring complex and long-term treatment often end up overwhelmed by debt. In 2021, Xi promised that the future would be healthy. But the level of investment this would involve, for 1.4 billion people, would rank this as one of the greatest administrative challenges facing any government in the world today.

This is compounded by the rapidly ageing population. The Xi government has already tried to encourage people to have more children, with very limited success. A second tactic – allowing migration from countries like India or elsewhere with surplus younger populations – is not even being considered at present, due to Chinese attitudes that verge on xenophobia.* Like Japan, China is experimenting with using robots to look after the rising number of elderly people. In 2013, the government even passed a law requiring that children visit their parents.[10] But such intervention is hardly sustainable. Decades of migrant labourers arriving from rural areas into the city and high levels of social mobility mean the family structure of today looks very different to that seen as recently as the 1990s. Years of dramatic economic growth have had a social cost; they were fuelled by people working in factories that were often hundreds of miles from their homes, their children brought up by other people. There is now additional conflict between those internal migrant workers who wish to settle permanently

---

* In April 2020, the Group of African Ambassadors wrote to China's foreign minister, protesting at the discrimination their countrymates were facing from the Chinese authorities during the spread of Covid-19, particularly in the southern city of Guangzhou.

in their new place of work and residence, and those who want to return to the place of their birth. Remarkably, China maintains the same internal passport system it has had in place since the 1950s – the *hukou*, or household registration document, which gives different, and better, privileges to those registered as being born in cities than to those from rural areas. Despite several attempts to reform this system by allowing some people to change their status, for many millions it remains a bureaucratic barrier, meaning they are considered temporary residents of a place where they may have lived for decades. By 2035, the year set by the 2021 resolution, this will have to be reformed. It is a major source of discontent to many Chinese.

Another crucial component of health is mental wellbeing. Before Xi, there was little talk of this, even though the country has had specialist mental health centres in Beijing and Shanghai since the 1980s. The Chinese have discovered, as their Western counterparts have, that capitalism can make you wealthier, and physically healthier, but it can also have a dramatic impact on your mental health. The envy and dissatisfaction that pervades Western social media and culture is now felt strongly in China too.[11] In a remarkable study of mental health in the country, Canadian based academic Jie Yang has written of the explosion of new mental health conditions: as there is socialism with Chinese characteristics, so too there are now neurosis with Chinese characteristics. Yang describes three in her book

– 'empty heart syndrome' for officials, 'princess syndrome' for young women and 'petitioner syndrome' for the social under-class. Each of these speaks to aspects of society that are unique to Xi's China. Officials, rich in power and surrounded by people who want their help, realise that they exist in an environment where everyone wants to use them, and no one likes them. Young women live in a country where there are 34 million more men than women, partly because of the distortions of the one-child policies of previous eras. For many of them, the choice of husband becomes so vexed that they demand stratospheric con-ditions – several apartments, huge wages, large dowries paid by one family to another (usually the wife's). Failure to find these almost impossible conditions results in a pathological response. There are numerous cases of young women cracking under the family and social pressures placed on them, resulting in tragic breakdowns, or, in the most extreme cases, suicide. There has been a striking rise in the number who chose to opt out of this and not marry at all. Finally, those who have failed to win civil court cases where they are trying to right grievances suffered as a result of official or corporate misbehaviour and subsequently repeatedly petition officials, experience constant frustration, mistreatment by the security agents hired to stop them caus-ing trouble and a sense of hopelessness as they realise they may never get redress; this can lead to breakdowns and severe depression. The provision of counselling and psychotherapy in China is limited or non-existent, depending on location. All too often, those who do break down are placed in asylums and heavily medicated. The Chinese government has recognised that this is unsustainable. But as with governments elsewhere, it also knows that resources are finite and that improving the situation might need almost limitless funds. If Xi wants to create a rich and healthy China by 2035, mental health provision must be a key part of his plan.

And then there is the challenge of the natural environment – how to repair a country whose physical landscape has been blighted by four decades of the most epic and fastest industrialisation a society has ever gone through. The difficulties here are well known – heavily polluted rivers, air that is almost poisonous to breathe, soil so contaminated that it can no longer safely grow crops. It was symbolic that, from 2012 to 2013, Beijing and other major cities were afflicted with a particularly heavy smog. Landing in the capital during this time, I remember the sensation of plunging from clear blue skies above the city into a thick porridge of cloud, in which it was impossible to see the ground beneath us. From one hotel, in the city centre, I was unable to see across the street to the adjacent skyscrapers, let alone catch sight of the Fragrant Hills, which were visible from the same spot on clear days in the past.

This smog was not merely an eyesore but had a real impact on the respiratory health of China's city dwellers. Bronchial and asthmatic diseases rocketed. The five-year plans set out in 2016 and 2021 were bravely labelled as 'green growth' plans by the government. A fundamental part of the China Dream is to live in cities with clean air and good quality water. But Xi cannot easily sacrifice economic growth for a wholly green economy. There has to be a transitional phase. The government has vowed that carbon emissions will peak by 2030, and that the country will be carbon neutral three decades after that. However, these aims are almost certainly not enough. Floods in 2021, similar to ones that blighted Germany in the same year, were largely attributed to the effect of climate change. The source of China's great rivers, the Yangtze and the Yellow River, are found in the Tibetan Plateau. Glacial melting here, and the resulting floods and disruption, is causing havoc. Hundreds of millions of people live in the impacted area. The Yellow River, with its constantly shifting course and the massive floods it has caused though a large swathe of central China throughout Chinese history, has sometimes been labelled 'China's sorrow'. Climate change could well be China's nemesis – a ticking time bomb, which, while it threatens submerging one part of the country under water, is causing droughts and a permanent lack of water in the north-east.

This list of issues affecting Chinese people looks remarkably similar to those that affect the average European or North American. They want a nice home, a clean and predictable living environment, a sense of security and wellbeing. They want to be able to walk down their local streets, or drive on them, without being threatened or mugged. They want rewarding, well-paid jobs and a pension when they retire. They want a reliable, affordable health service. Despite the screen of politics through which they are often seen, if the China of the future delivers on these promises, it means, ironically, that China will look like the rest of the world – on the surface, at least.

The Communists have often presented themselves as architects of the future. If one wants to see what that future might look like, one should visit Shanghai, where, in many ways, it has already arrived. Before the pandemic, the shops there heaved with people. The streets were clogged with cars, many of them luxury brands, and the subway was extensive, mostly new and, even more staggering for someone used to the London Underground, effectively air-conditioned, despite the frequently sweltering temperatures outside. Shanghai carries a very convincing veneer of internationalisation. It has shopping malls full of familiar products, and people are dressed in the same swish, cutting-edge fashion brands one might see in New York or Paris. There is no sense of cultural cringe here, but of a city rushing with open arms towards the future. Where there were once farmland and warehouses, there now stands the world's second tallest skyscraper, the Shanghai Tower. One can have tea in one of the world's highest hotels, the Grand

Hyatt, though these days it stands behind a cluster of even more gargantuan structures. In the Xintiandi centre, one can walk in restored heritage streets, visit old-fashioned tea shops or restaurants and sample cuisine from any of the country's regions, or from Japan, Thailand, Italy or France. The city is, however, like a mirage. As economist Yasheng Huang pointed out over a decade ago in his excellent book, *Capitalism with Chinese Characteristics*, the vast majority of Shanghai's economy is in the hands of the state. The great Pudong financial development was mostly achieved through landgrab and evicting farmers so that new development could happen.[12] Even so, the energy and sheer passion of the place never ceases to impress me. In 2015, I was invited to debate against Huang, for a conference the *Economist* organised in the city. We had a good discussion about whether the city would become a global technology centre. Huang made a number of powerful points, full of data and evidence to show that Shanghai talked the talk but would never walk the walk. My reply was that this city would always be conquering the future, through the spirit of its people and the way it captured the imaginations of both its own inhabitants and of outsiders. Despite the barriers Huang set out, if it had the will, it would find a way, I argued. In that debate I just about won the audience over by a small margin, despite Huang's formidable opposition. In 2021, despite the terrible record of outsiders trying to predict where China might be going, and what its future holds, I would still give the country a good chance of bringing about a large part of its China Dream. Even in the depths of 2022, with no immediate end in sight for the Covid-19 pandemic, my faith in China, under Xi or whoever else one day replaces him, being able to surmount the formidable challenges facing it, and creating its own unique version of modernity, is still strong. And what a world that might be – where the whole of China buzzes with the energy and life of the great city of Shanghai. But by that time, Shanghai will already be well on the way to super modernity, monopolising the future, taunting the outside world to try to catch up.

Afterword: Who is Xi?

Were Chinese politics to follow the path of the past 30 years, then in 2022, after two full five-year terms of the Xi leadership, there would be widespread speculation about who his successor is likely to be. A decade in power was the time allowed Jiang Zemin and Hu Jintao. However, with Xi at this mark, we find ourselves in a different situation. He looks set to stay well beyond the Twentieth Party Congress scheduled for late 2022. The only impediment to this is his health and age – he will be 70 in 2023 – and unexpected events that might happen in China or the wider world, impacting on the country and causing his, and the party's, removal.

Disasters cannot be discounted. Covid-19 threatened to be one of these. But a semi-perpetual leadership is still the strongest and most likely current outcome. Like Putin, Xi may be with us deep into the 2030s. An assessment of his future role today, therefore, can be only highly provisional. Nevertheless, so far we have a decade of events, responses and revelations – of a sort – about his world view and his style of leadership.

Compared to the eight years maximum allotted a US president, this is plenty to go on.

It is worth remembering the comments made by the nameless American-based individual who had known Xi in his youth, which were published by WikiLeaks in 2009. Long before Xi ever figured as a main leader in China, when he was only the first among many contenders, and it was likely he might be sidelined and supplanted, the acquaintance noted that while Xi was not corruptible by money or material goods, he might be corrupted by power. We now have a pretty good basis of evidence to assess if this is the case.

Questions about the nature of Xi's power have recurred throughout this book. Answering them is not helped by the fact that the Chinese system privileges opacity. This has been part of the culture of the Communist Party since its days as an underground, subversive force. The trauma of the era in which it had to fight for its existence has left a profound mark on its memory. Throughout the Mao years, even when it had all the main levers of power at hand, paranoia was never far away. The party grew adept at outlining who its enemies were, and how they needed to be managed. Even the most loyal were swept away in some of these campaigns. Since the Deng era, while a huge effort has gone into institutionalising the processes of the party – holding more regular, predictable congresses and other kinds of meetings, more structure about

how cadres are assessed, diversifying and widening membership and defining party and other government functions – in
the end, context, pragmatism and necessity trumps all else.
If the situation demands a specific set of responses for the
party to stay in power and see off organised opposition, then,
broadly, anything goes. For the 1990s and 2000s, a more collegial leadership structure was needed, as China found its feet
economically on the international stage. But China's position
is now very different. The state and country have far greater
resources. The message of national rejuvenation is unifying,
and tangible. The onus today is on maintaining focus, on not
screwing things up and throwing this historic chance away.

Xi's powers are intimately defined and shaped by those of
the party. The Communist Party itself is a strategising body.
That strategising must decide on the type of leadership and
what role it plays in prevailing over the challenges facing the
country. Of course, this can go wrong. If we look at Mao, we
can see that over the 1950s and into the 1960s he grew increasingly frustrated with the leadership format given to him by the
party. The Cultural Revolution was, on one level, an attempt
to subvert and change this. Ultimately, though, with the rise
of Deng, the party prevailed, even against Mao.

When structured in a successful way, leadership can
articulate the party's priorities with one voice, and achieve the
great alchemy of transforming ideology into practical edicts.

For these reasons, Leadership with a capital 'L' has become an institution within the party in China. Much as there is an Office of the President of the United States with a whole army of enablers and administrators largely invisible to public view, so China has created an Office of the Party Secretary and President, from whom others can derive their authority to act. In a complex, often labyrinthine system, calling for policies in the name of the president and party leader gets things done. In a sense, it creates a power franchise, where others are able to act through delegated powers.

One of the striking developments in the Xi leadership style is the ways in which the premier, usually the second most powerful figure in the set-up, has been pushed into the background. The name of Xi's current deputy, Premier Li Keqiang, has figured very little in this book. In studies of Hu or Jiang or Mao, their respective premiers Wen Jiabao, Zhu Rongji and Zhou Enlai were all immensely significant. This is not the case with Li. Even the usual guiding role the premier has over the economy has been scaled down so that all major issues in this realm have been shifted to the more political side of decision making. In a sense, that reflects the fact that economics for the party today are merely another political tool. Like social policy, and healthcare, economics takes its place in delivering one common objective – sustainable one-party rule. Xi is the chief politician in this system. Therefore, he is also the chief person in command of everything – from the military to the markets.

There is one problem that Xi is in place to solve, and by which history will judge him: to make party rule perpetual. Achieving that would mean that China has succeeded where the USSR failed. It would upend the so-called laws of modernity, which state that only a democracy can control a successful, large, middle-income economy. In order to attain this goal, almost anything is justifiable. Much of Xi's authority and power derives from the fact that it is he who is ruling China at the moment when this objective of the party is closer to realisation than ever before. At a time of such promise and culmination, failure is not an option. Because many in the outside world do not regard this objective either as desirable nor possible, they do not understand the appeal Xi holds for his party colleagues and the Chinese people more broadly.

Where Xi has shown true innovation and acted differently to his predecessors is in international affairs. He has diverged from the low-key, almost silent style of Hu. Even so, this is not surprising. None of Xi's predecessors had the advantage of a country with such a huge economy and so many material strengths in terms of military, space and technological assets. Whether they wanted to or not, previous leaders were not able to spell out a Chinese global vision. The closest any of them came to one was, perhaps, Mao's Third World idea, announced by Deng Xiaoping during one of his brief rehabilitations in the early 1970s. However, that notion was more about carving up the world so that China had space to face its two opponents, America and the USSR. Xi's Belt and Road Initiative is designed to embrace anyone who wants to join with it, rather than reject specific nations. That neither Japan nor America has opted to join it is their choice. Globalisation with Chinese characteristics is a new outcome, arising from a new situation. It is also an admission by the Xi leadership that China's domestic fate is intimately tied to its international situation.

The production values of the whole performance are of high quality. The projected image of Xi is of the leader a country deserves when it is the world's second largest power, waiting until it can occupy the pinnacle itself. Xi's propagandists have been helped by the other global leaders currently in power. Trump's unique style of speaking and divisive personality made Xi look coherent and authoritative. European leaders either lacked the profile Trump enjoyed or followed Trump's lead and ended up making Xi look comparatively competent. It is no minor point that China's responses to various UK-originated criticisms of its actions in Hong Kong have become sharper and more dismissive since 2016, as its diplomats watched the struggles to deliver Brexit and the various dramatic contortions in the politics of their old adversary.

The way Xi uses language has also had a strong impact, both domestically and internationally. In his early years in power his style was clipped and direct. Phrases like 'China Dream' were repeated ad nauseum. The notion of party values and of the mission of China under Xi's rule to be a great rejuvenated nation were hammered home at every possible opportunity. He avoided using heavy doses of ideological language, choosing to tell stories instead. The dense use of statistics was also jettisoned. Optimism was stressed – China was entering the New Era, where all challenges could be solved, and every day offered a new opportunity. Trust was created by solemn pledges to strike hard against corruption. These words were put into action when significant figures were dramatically taken in and made examples of. Xi was the man who said he would do things, and honoured his word. Obama's winning 2008 election campaign used the phrase, 'Yes we can'. In Xi's China a similar sense of purposefulness is present. All of this was manifested in the confident, expansive and fluent way in which Xi spoke, not just to China, but to the wider world. Chinese people could see images of him travelling the world, unafraid to speak on an equal basis with other global leaders. It is noticeable, though, that the longer he has been in power, the more verboseness has crept back in.*

---

* Witness the epic three-and-a-half-hour speech at the 2017 Party Congress.

Beyond all this, though, acknowledgement has to be given to Xi's political instincts. He may be acting out a role written by the party, but he is playing it well. He has often spoken about comprehensiveness; he needs to see the bigger picture, being the one person who can sit atop the vast edifice, see all that is going on and offer some form of strategic direction. Xi is the sole head of the military, the party and the state. He heads many other things too. As conductor-in-chief, to use his own metaphor, even he has limits. He can't create new instruments or invent new ways of performing. But he can decide tempo and volume. He must prioritise the main tasks that China has to do, as a conductor draws out a melody. Disciplining the party was essential, just as a conductor needs players who are able to keep time and play in tune. Similar discipline had to be enforced in the military, the media and business. Focussing on the development of the needs of the middle class and strengthening their legal and financial situation had to be prioritised because of their importance in making China a middle-income country. It also meant, somewhat more problematically, that any disruption to the goal of becoming a middle-income country had to be controlled – most notably in Hong Kong and Xinjiang. Xi made the most of the opportunities proffered him, responding to the challenges of the Trump era, and then Covid-19, reshaping the main strategic goals so that they run in a slightly different way. As of 2022, Xi has managed to get the priorities right. The country has not been beset by disaster. The show has gone on. That, in view of the complexities of the task facing him, is no small feat.

There are storm clouds on the horizon though. As of 2022, Xi's style of power and leadership poses problems in three areas: over-promising, overreaching and over-idealising. Xi's 2017 Party Congress speech and the 2021 resolution were replete with promises. Some of Xi's speeches read like a uto-pian statement along the lines of William Morris' *News from Nowhere*, where the future is only ever bright and the sunshine here to stay. But in almost every area where these promises were being made, there were trade-offs: vast resources were involved, huge financial and business vested interests were provoked and there were real risks of poor implementation. Policies around mental health, healthcare, pensions and the environment were the most problematic. Failure to keep up with the delivery of some of the many promises will quickly burn up what credit Xi and the party has with the great emerg-ing middle class, who are crucial for the party's future and its legitimacy. The China Dream will turn into the China Nightmare if things go badly wrong in any of these areas.

Overreach is the corollary of this. The party under Xi is doing too much, and doing it too intensively. One example is the much-heralded and commented-on social credit system. Envisaged as a national network covering almost every citizen and allowing immense predictive and controlling range to the authorities, in 2021 its implementation remained confusing and patchy. In principle, the idea is not difficult. People are assigned scores for debt, misbehaviour and failure to pay taxes or fines. This is not so different to the rubrics used by debt agencies and insurers in the West. However, the concern was that because China has zero meaningful legal data protection, the party was theoretically able to gather even more information on the lives of its citizens. The lack of clarity from the central government about how local officials were meant to roll out the programme, and a host of technical and other problems, showed that incorporating 1.4 billion people in one network was not straightforward.

Then there is the final issue – Xi and the party's habit to idealise. The greatest tragedies and mistakes of the past seven decades of party rule in China have derived not from malign intent but the precise opposite – good intentions gone awry. It was not Mao Zedong's intention to see many millions of his own people starve during the famines of the early 1960s. Reportedly, when he became aware of the suffering rural China was enduring, he was devastated and uncomprehending. The same goes for the Cultural Revolution from 1966; Mao's utopianism, the establishment of communes and the cleansing of class ranks all looked sensible and beneficial, on paper at least. The miserable social and personal impact of this was only apparent once the clean theory was translated into messier practice. Deng Xiaoping was less prone to such pure ideals, but even he, in 1989, was unapologetic about placing the party needs above those of anyone else – its prime function was to deliver what he regarded an increasingly perfected society, which only the party was able to do. His conviction meant tolerating dissent, such as that in Tiananmen Square, was impossible.

Idealism has always lurked in the body politic of modern China. Xi shows this too, when he slips into the language of the New Era, where everything will be better, bigger, faster. His vision is of a China that is clean, rich and full of happy, fulfilled people. By 2049, Xi's refrain goes, the country will be a democratic, developed, prosperous one (though with the important qualifier that this democracy will be 'with Chinese characteristics'). Its economy will overshadow all others. It will be restored to its historic status as a great, strong, powerful country. The dream will have come true. But one has to wonder, what happens to the party after that? What is its function then? It will have done what it set out to achieve. Will it be disbanded? Will it morph into some other shape? One thing is certain: if China ever does get to this point, the party will need to radically change to justify its continued power. That will prove to be the hardest challenge of all. It may well be insurmountable.

I have described Xi as an actor performing in a drama written by the party, to convey the crucial, complex relationship that Xi has with the party of which he is a part. He cannot be understood outside of this relationship. As of 2022, to his audience in the party, and among many Chinese people, his act has been good enough. But there is one element of this performance that has become increasingly unsettling. Bit by bit, what was once a more fully peopled stage has slowly lost most of its other players. Supporting acts, members of the chorus and co-leads have gone. Some exited dramatically – figures like Bo Xilai. Others seemed to fade gradually – Wang Qishan comes to mind; in 2022 he barely figures in the party despite his previous influence. Military, artistic and media figures – like the tennis player Peng Shuai, who, after claiming she had been sexually harassed by a former top-level leader Zhang Gaoli, confusingly disappeared and then reappeared in 2021, or Alibaba's Jack Ma Yun, who suffered a similar period of silencing – have all seen their roles either reduced, or, in some cases, written out of the plot altogether. Will we end up with a one-man show? And will that really be enough to carry the enormity of the drama that China is today and will be in the decade ahead? At some point, will the audience watching from the dark amphitheatre grow tired? And if that point comes, how will the one-man show end? All we know is that Xi's name is still up in lights. They haven't dimmed yet. The problem is, when they do, turmoil and uncertainty in China will reach deep into the outside world. Like it or not, the drama the party has written, and that Xi is playing – comedy or tragedy, happy or unhappy ending – is one that, wherever we are, we will have to keep on watching. We are all Xi's audience now.

Notes

Chapter One: Xi Jinping: The Enigma of Chinese Power

1. Frederick Teiwes and Warren Sun, *The End of the Maoist Era: Chinese Politics During the Twilight of the Cultural Revolution, 1972–1976* (New York: Routledge, 2007) offers a good example.

2. Zheng Yongnian, *The Chinese Communist Party as Organisational Emperor.* (London: Routledge, 2010).

3. James Fallows and Caroline Kitchener, 'Xi Reveals Himself as an Autocrat', *Atlantic*, 26 February 2018.

4. Kapil Komireddi, 'Senator Marco Rubio says business-as-usual with Beijing is "not an option"', *The Critic*, 17 March 2021.

5. David Charter, 'China is a threat to democratic way of life, says Joe Biden at summit', *The Times*, 9 December 2021.

6. 'EU–China Relations factsheet', European External Action Service, 20 June 2020, https://eeas.europa.eu/topics/external-investment-plan/34728/eu-china-relations-.

7. Tessa Wong, 'Sinophobia: How a virus reveals the many ways China is feared', BBC News, 20 February 2020, https://www.bbc.co.uk/news/world-asia-51456056.

8. Kiyoshi Ota, 'World Cup glory is Xi Jinping's dream for China', *The Conversation*, 17 June 2018, https://theconversation.com/world-cup-glory-is-xi-jinpings-dream-for-china-96750.

9. A minority of scientists have hypothesised that the virus may have been created by mistake in a laboratory specialising in the study of this area in Wuhan and then unintentionally transmitted to the outside world; on that the consensus is undecided, as of December 2021.

10. 'China: Overview', Coronavirus Resource Center, Johns Hopkins University, https://coronavirus.jhu.edu/region/china.

11. 'America: Overview', Coronavirus Resource Center, Johns Hopkins University, https://coronavirus.jhu.edu/region/united-states, and 'COVID-19 Data Repository by the Center for Systems Science and Engineering (CSSE) at Johns Hopkins University', Johns Hopkins University, https://github.com/CSSEGISandData/COVID-19.

12. 'Xi Jinping: From princeling to president', BBC News, 12 May 2021, https://www.bbc.co.uk/news/world-asia-pacific-11551399.

13. For claims of Chinese influence in American, British and Australian politics, see Clive Hamilton and Mareike Ohlberg, *Hidden Hand: Exposing How the Chinese Communist Party Is Reshaping the World* (London: One World Publications, 2020).

14. Charles Moore, 'Jesus College's China problem', *Spectator*, 1 August 2020.

15. See for instance, Jack Stubbs, 'Britain says Huawei security failings pose long-term risk: govt report', Reuters, 1 October 2020, https://www.reuters.com/article/us-britain-huawei-idUSKBN26M64S and Timothy Nerozzi, 'Biden admin says Huawei is "national security threat"', Fox News, 15 December 2021, https://www.foxbusiness.com/politics/biden-admin-huawei-national-security-threat.

16. Yen Nee Lee, 'Escalating EU-China tensions could jeopardize new investment deal', CNBC, 23 March 2021, https://www.cnbc.com/2021/03/23/retaliatory-eu-china-sanctions-could-jeopardize-new-investment-deal.html.

17. 'Canada's parliament declares China's treatment of Uighurs "genocide"', BBC News, 23 February 2021, https://www.bbc.co.uk/news/world-us-canada-56163220.

18. 'China: More than 300 rights lawyers detained in nationwide crackdown, including lawyers who handled cases on corporate abuses; at least 6 face formal charges', Business and Human Rights Resource Centre, 13 July 2015, https://www.business-humanrights.org/en/latest-news/china-more-than-300-rights-lawyers-detained-in-nationwide-crackdown-including-lawyers-who-handled-cases-on-corporate-abuses-at-least-6-face-formal-charges/.

19. 'Big data, meet Big Brother: China invents the digital totalitarian state', *Economist*, 17 December 2016.

20. 'Chairman of everything', *The Economist*, 2 April 2016, https://www.economist.com/china/2016/04/02/chairman-of-everything.

21. 'The World's Top 100 Universities', QS, https://www.topuniversities.com/student-info/choosing-university/worlds-top-100-universities.

22. Willy Wo-Lap Lam, *Chinese Politics in the Era of Xi Jinping*. (New York and London: Routledge, 2015), p. 48.

Chapter Two: The Xi Story – 1953–2002

1. While the Chinese government in the past have officially recognised that up to 20 million died, scholar Yang Jisheng in his epic *Tombstone: The Great Chinese Famine 1958–1962* (Ed. Edward Friedman, trans Guo Jian and Stacy Mosher, London and New York: Penguin, 2013) has an estimate of 36 million upwards. The disparity is as much about how lack of adequate food, while not being the ultimate cause of deaths, certainly exacerbates existing conditions.

2. These are given in a Chinese language collection of eyewitness accounts issued in 2017: *Xi Jinping de Qi Nian Zhiqing Suiyue (Xi Jinping's Seven Years as a Sent Down Youth)* (Beijing: Central Party School Publishing House, 2017).

3. The material here is taken from *Xi Jinping de Qi Nian Zhiqing Suiyue (Xi Jinping's Seven Years as a Sent Down Youth)* (Beijing: Central Party School Publishing House, 2017).

4. Covell Meyskens, 'Document about model worker Xi Jinping from 1975', Everyday Life in Mao's China, https://everydaylifeinmaoistchina.org/2021/09/14/document-about-model-worker-xi-jinping-from-1975/

5. Lance Gore, *Chinese Politics Illustrated: The Cultural, Social and Historical Context* (Singapore: World Scientific, 2014), pp. 10–11.

6. Ibid., p. 18.

7. J.T. Quigley, 'Lee Kuan Yew Compares Xi Jinping to Nelson Mandela in New Book', *Diplomat*, 8 August 2013, https://thediplomat.com/2013/08/lee-kuan-yew-compares-xi-jinping-to-nelson-mandela-in-new-book/.

8. Gore, *Chinese Politics Illustrated*, p. 19.

9. Joseph Torigian, 'Xi Jinping's Tiananmen Family Lessons', Foreign Policy, 4 June 2020, https://foreignpolicy.com/2020/06/04/xi-jinping-tiananmen-lessons-chinese-communist-party/.

Chapter Three: The Zhejiang Years – 2002–2007

1. Rowan Callick, *Party Time* (New York: Basic Books, 2013).

2. Kjeld Erik Brødsgaard, 'Cadres and Personnel Management in the CPC', *China: An International Journal* 10.2 (2012): 69–83, 72.

3. 'China's Provincial Economies: Growing Together or Pulling Apart?', Moody's Analytics, January 2019, https://www.moodysanalytics.com/-/media/article/2019/china-provincial-economies.pdf.

4. 'Alibaba IPO: Jack Ma's Original Sales Pitch in 1999', Bloomberg Quicktake, YouTube, 8 September 2014, https://www.youtube.com/watch?v=Up9-C4_8dVo.

5. Jonathan Kaiman, 'China's "Brother Wristwatch" Yang Dacai jailed for 14 years for corruption', *Guardian*, 5 September 2013, https://www.theguardian.com/world/2013/sep/05/china-brother-wristwatch-yang-dacai-sentenced.

6. 'Corrupt Chinese Official Felled by 11 Mistresses', Reuters, 7 September 2007, https://www.reuters.com/article/us-china-mistresses-odd-idUSPEK36711520070907.

7. Edward Cody, 'Chinese Police Bring Villagers To Heel After Latest Uprising', *Washington Post*, 21 December 2005, https://www.washingtonpost.com/archive/politics/2005/12/21/chinese-police-bring-villagers-to-heel-after-latest-uprising/c26fa04a-2a83-4a0e-acc0-f64a86358c41/.

8. Chinese National Bureau of Statistics, 'Main Data of the Seventh National Population Census', 11 May 2021, http://www.stats.gov.cn/english/PressRelease/202105/t20210510_1817185.html.

9. Xi Jinping, *The Governance of China*, Volume 3 (Beijing: Foreign Language Press, 2020), p. 94.

10. 'PORTRAIT OF VICE PRESIDENT XI JINPING: "AMBITIOUS SURVIVOR" OF THE CULTURAL REVOLUTION', WikiLeaks, 16 November 2006, https://wikileaks.org/plusd/cables/09BEIJING3128_a.html.

Chapter Four: Xi in the Centre: His Time in Power – 2007–2017

1. Mao Yushi, *Where has the Anxiety of the Chinese Come From* (Shanghai: Qunyuan Books, 2013).

2. Eric Reeves, 'China, Darfur, and the 2008 Summer Olympics: An Intolerable Contradiction', E-International Relations, 20 April 2008,

https://www.e-ir.info/2008/04/20/china-darfur-and-the-2008-summer-olympics-an-intolerable-contradiction/.

3. See, for instance, Clifford Coonan, 'Mystery of Xi Jinping's two weeks in hiding', *Independent*, 2 November 2012.

4. 'Xi Jinping's Chongqing Tour: Gang of Princelings Gains Clout', Jamestown Foundation, 17 December 2010, https://jamestown.org/program/xi-jinpings-chongqing-tour-gang-of-princelings-gains-clout/.

5. Charles Hutzler, 'China police chief sought asylum in US, says Chinese media', *Christian Science Monitor*, 19 September 2012, https://www.csmonitor.com/World/Latest-News-Wires/2012/0919/China-police-chief-sought-asylum-in-US-says-Chinese-media.

6. 'Murdered Briton Neil Heywood's mother in China appeal', BBC News, 12 August 2013, https://www.bbc.co.uk/news/world-asia-china-23662795.

7. 'Top Chinese officials "plotted to overthrow Xi Jinping"', BBC News, 20 October 2017, https://www.bbc.co.uk/news/world-asia-china-41691917.

8. Jamil Anderlini, 'Beijing on Edge Amid Coup Rumours', *Financial Times*, 21 March 2012.

9. David Barboza, 'Billions in Hidden Riches for Family of Chinese Leader', *New York Times*, 25 October 2012.

10. 'Full text: China's new party chief Xi Jinping's speech', BBC News, 15 November 2012, https://www.bbc.co.uk/news/world-asia-china-20338586.

11. 'Xi shows common touch with visit to bun eatery', *China Daily*, 31 December 2013.

12. Matthew Timms, 'Chinese five-star hotels fight to downgrade as luxury is shunned', Business Destinations, 5 June 2014, https://www.businessdestinations.com/relax/hotels/chinese-five-star-hotels-fight-to-downgrade-as-luxury-is-shunned/.

13. 'Four Dishes and One Soup', *China Economic Review*, 22 January 2013, https://chinaeconomicreview.com/four-dishes-one-soup/.

14. Sean Silbert, 'Given glimpse into Xi Jinping's daily life, China goes gaga', *Los Angeles Times*, 27 October 2014.

15. Xi, *The Governance of China*, Volume 3, p. 170.

16. *The Story of Shenzhen*, United Nations Human Settlements Programme, 2019, Nairobi, https://www.metropolis.org/sites/default/files/resources/the_story_of_shenzhen_2nd_edition_sep_2019_0.pdf, p. 3.

17. 'Hu Jintao visits county to promote ideological campaign, *People's Daily*, 18 November 2008, http://en.people.cn/90001/90776/90785/6535378.html.

18. Xi Jinping, *The Governance of China*, Volume 1 (Beijing: Foreign Language Press, 2014), p. 37.

19. Ibid., p. 27.

20. 'Profile: Xi Jinping: Man of the people, statesman of vision', *China Daily*, 24 December 2012.

21. 'PORTRAIT OF VICE PRESIDENT XI JINPING: "AMBITIOUS SURVIVOR" OF THE CULTURAL REVOLUTION', WikiLeaks, 16 November 2009, https://wikileaks.org/plusd/cables/09BEIJING3128_a.html.

22. Tania Branigan, 'Xi Jinping Vows to Fight Tigers and Flies in Anti-corruption Drive', *Guardian*, 22 January 2013.

23. Andrew Wedeman, *Double Paradox: Rapid Growth and Rising Corruption in China* (New York: Cornell University Press, 2012).

24. Xu Zhangrun, 'Viral Alarm: When Fury Overcomes Fear', translated by Geremie Barmé, 10 February 2020, China File, https://www.chinafile.com/reporting-opinion/viewpoint/viral-alarm-when-fury-overcomes-fear.

25. Josh Rudolph, 'Loyal party members urge Xi's resignation', China Digital Times, 16 March 2016, https://chinadigitaltimes.net/2016/03/open-letter-devoted-party-members-urge-xis-resignation/.

26. 'China's per capita GDP crosses $10,000-mark for the first time', Business Standard, 17 January 2020, https://www.business-standard.com/article/pti-stories/china-s-per-capita-gdp-crosses-usd-10-000-mark-for-the-first-time-120011701060_1.html.

27. Gerard A. Postiglione, 'Expanding Higher Education', *China Quarterly*, Volume 244 (December 2020), pp. 920–41, p. 923.

28. 'Privately owned vehicle number in China 2009–2019', Statista, 29 October 2021, https://www.statista.com/statistics/278475/privately-owned-vehicles-in-china/#:~:text=In%202019%2C%20approximately%20225.09%20million,cars%20were%20registered%20in%20China.

29. Xi, *The Governance of China*, Volume 1, p. 78.

30. 'China's economy grows 6.7% in 2016', BBC News, 20 January 2017, https://www.bbc.co.uk/news/business-38686568.

31. World Bank, https://data.worldbank.org/indicator/NE.GDI.FTOT.ZS?locations=CNandhttps://data.worldbank.org/indicator/NE.CON.TOTL.ZS?locations=CN.

32. World Bank, https://data.worldbank.org/indicator/NE.CON.TOTL.ZS?locations=US.

33. Dan Harsha, 'Taking China's Pulse', *Harvard Gazette*, 9 July 2020, https://news.harvard.edu/gazette/story/2020/07/long-term-survey-reveals-chinese-government-satisfaction/.

34. Perhaps the most concise presentation of this argument is by the UK Uyghur Tribunal of 2021, whose final judgment (albeit an unofficial one unrecognised by either the UK or Chinese government) can be found here: https://uyghurtribunal.com/wp-content/uploads/2021/12/Uyghur-Tribunal-Summary-Judgment-9th-Dec-21.pdf.

35. 'Inside Xinjiang's Prison State', *New Yorker*, 26 February 2021.

Chapter Five: Xi and the New Era – 2017–2021

1. 'China's luxury cars see sales surge in 2020', China.org, 2 February 2021, http://www.china.org.cn/business/2021-02/02/content_77179184.htm.

2. Tom Phillips, 'Xi Jinping heralds "new era" of Chinese power at Communist party congress', *Guardian*, 18 October 2017.

3. 'Xi Jinping has more clout than Donald Trump. The world should be wary', *Economist*, 14 October 2017.

4. David Runciman, *Politics: Ideas in Profile* (London: Profile Books, 2014).

5. 'China adopts intelligence law', Xinhua, 27 June 2017, http://www.xinhuanet.com//english/2017-06/27/c_136398422.htm.

6. Bonnie Girard, 'The Real Danger of China's National Intelligence Law', *Diplomat*, 23 February 2019, https://thediplomat.com/2019/02/the-real-danger-of-chinas-national-intelligence-law/.

7. Larry Diamond, 'Why East Asia – Including China – Will Turn Democratic Within a Generation', *Atlantic*, 24 January 2012, https://www.theatlantic.com/international/archive/2012/01/why-east-asia-including-china-will-turn-democratic-within-a-generation/251824/.

8. See 'China's Threat to Democracies Around the World', Democracy Works Podcast, https://www.democracyworkspodcast.com/china/.

Chapter Six: Xi and the World – 2022

1. Bill Hayton, *The Invention of China* (New Haven: Yale University Press, 2020).

2. Alex W. Palmer, 'The Man Behind China's Aggressive New Voice', *New York Times*, 7 July 2021, https://www.nytimes.com/2021/07/07/magazine/china-diplomacy-twitter-zhao-lijian.html.

3. 'Chinese riot after Japan win final', CNN, 8 August 2004, http://edition.cnn.com/2004/SPORT/football/08/07/china.japan/.

4. 'China table tennis boss complains Olympic playing areas too small', Japan Today, 20 July 2021, https://japantoday.com/category/tokyo-2020-olympics/china-table-tennis-boss-says-olympic-playing-areas-too-small.

5. AFP, 'China becoming "evil empire" warns US ex-VP Mike Pence', Hong Kong Free Press, 15 July 2021, https://hongkongfp.com/2021/07/15/china-becoming-evil-empire-warns-us-ex-vp-mike-pence/.

6. Nick Gass, 'Chinese president, visiting US, makes a "House of Cards" joke', Politico, 23 September 2015, https://www.politico.com/story/2015/09/xi-jinping-house-of-cards-joke-213961.

7. Ben Blanchard and John Ruwitch, 'China hikes defense budget, to spend more on internal security', Reuters, 5 March 2013, https://www.reuters.com/article/us-china-parliament-defence-idUSBRE92403620130305.

8. Press Association, 'China rejects criticism from UK and allies over Hong Kong', *National*, 19 November 2020, https://www.thenational.scot/news/uk-news/18883847.china-rejects-criticism-uk-allies-hong-kong/.

9. A survey in 2021 showed that nearly 90 per cent of the island's inhabitants see themselves as Taiwanese, not Chinese. See Chen Yu-fu and Jonathan Chin, 'Nearly 90 percent of public identify with Taiwan: poll', *Taipei Times*, 11 August 2021, https://www.taipeitimes.com/News/front/archives/2021/08/11/2003762406.

10. Gagandeep Singh Dhillon, '154 self-immolations in Tibet since 2009, says Tibetan govt-in-exile', *India Express*, 22 February 2020, https://indianexpress.com/article/cities/shimla/154-self-immolations-in-tibet-since-2009-says-tibetan-govt-in-exile-6281835/#:~:text=26%20last%20year.-,%E2%80%9CTibetans%20continue%20to%20set%20their%20bodies%20ablaze%20to%20protest%20against,to%20have%20died%2C%20it%20said.

11. 'Uyghur Tribunal Judgment', Uyghur Tribunal, 9 December 2021, https://uyghurtribunal.com/wp-content/uploads/2021/12/Uyghur-Tribunal-Summary-Judgment-9th-Dec-21.pdf, p. 63.

12. Jessica C. Liao, 'How BRI Debt Puts China at Risk', The Diplomat, 27 October 2021, https://thediplomat.com/2021/10/how-bri-debt-puts-china-at-risk/.

13. Karl Mathiesen, 'China lost global leadership claims at COP26, says ex-Maldives president', Politico, 7 November 2021, https://www.politico.eu/article/china-global-leadership-cop26-maldives-president-mohamed-nasheed/.

14. Alan Rappeport, 'Trump Calls China a "Threat to the World" as Trade Talks Approach', *New York Times*, 20 September 2019.

15. Mark Moore, 'China's President Xi Jinping warns bullies will "face broken heads and bloodshed"', *New York Post*, 1 July 2021, https://nypost.com/2021/07/01/chinas-xi-warns-bullies-will-face-broken-heads-and-bloodshed/.

Chapter Seven: Xi and the Future

1. '2022 New Year address by President Xi Jinping', 31 December 2021, Ministry of Foreign Affairs of the People's Republic of China, https://www.fmprc.gov.cn/mfa_eng/zxxx_662805/202112/t20211231_10478096.html.

2. 'Full Text Resolution of the CPC Central Committee on the Major Achievements and Historical Experience of the Party over the Past Century', Xinhua, 16 November 2021, http://www.news.cn/english/2021-11/16/c_1310314611.htm.

3. 'Full Text of Chinese Communist Party's Resolution on History', Nikkei Asia, 19 November 2021, https://asia.nikkei.com/Politics/Full-text-of-the-Chinese-Communist-Party-s-new-resolution-on-history.

4. 'China House Prices Growth: 1999–2021', CEIC Data, https://www.ceicdata.com/en/indicator/china/house-prices-growth.

5. 'Beijing Population 2022', World Population Review, https://worldpopulationreview.com/world-cities/beijing-population.

6. Edward Glaeser, Wei Huang, Yueran Ma and Andrei Shleifer, 'A Real Estate Boom with Chinese Characteristics', *Journal of Economic Perspectives* (Winter 2017), https://scholar.harvard.edu/files/shleifer/files/jep_2017.pdf

7. Ibid.

8. 'Life expectancy at birth, male (years) – China', World Bank, https://data. worldbank.org/indicator/SP.DYN.LE00.MA.IN?locations=CN.

9. 'Current health expenditure (% of GDP) – United Kingdom, United States, China', World Bank, https://data.worldbank.org/indicator/SH. XPD.CHEX.GD.ZS?locations=GB-US-CN.

10. Celia Hatton, 'New China law says children "must visit parents"', BBC News, 1 July 2013, https://www.bbc.co.uk/news/world-asia-china-2312 4345.

11. Jie Yang, *Mental Health in China: Change, Tradition, and Therapeutic Governance* (London: Wiley, 2017).

12. Yasheng Huang, *Capitalism with Chinese Characteristics: Entrepreneurship and the State* (Cambridge: Cambridge University Press, 2008). The chapter entitled 'What is Wrong with Shanghai?' shows the faults and issues that lie beneath the surface of this great city.

Acknowledgements

I would like to express my gratitude to Clare Bullock and the team at Icon books for commissioning and then seeing this book to completion, and to the copy-editor James Lilford and proofreader Hanna Milner for the work they did on improving my original draft.

This book is dedicated to the memory of Frank Charles Clary, 1936–1994.

Index

INDEX

INDEX